Structural Challenges and the Future of Honors Education

Honors Education in Transition

Series Editor: **Robert W. Glover and Katherine M. O'Flaherty**

The landscape of American higher education has changed in notable ways in recent decades. One essential and defining feature of contemporary higher education is the growth of honors education. Honors education offers a means to student self-development, allowing high-performing students a distinctive venue in which they can pursue self-cultivation through expanded educational opportunities. This edited series engages a series of important and timely questions related to the contemporary state of honors education and what promises and challenges exist in its future development.

The first volume in the series engages with the growth in honors education generally, examining the culture around honors education and the challenges and opportunities created by its rapid growth. The second volume in the series turns to curriculum, exploring the various ways that honors educators pursue curricular innovations while navigating the tension between reverence for the past and pedagogical dynamism. The final volume considers how honors education can face larger structural dynamics in higher education—the push for online education, calls to demonstrate "return on investment," and market-based pressures to focus attention on specific fields and skills. Throughout, the series draws upon the insights of seasoned veterans of honors education and new voices to actively consider the future of this important and rapidly growing educational movement.

Titles in the Series

Present Successes and Future Challenges in Honors Education
Continuity and Innovation in Honors College Curricula
Structural Challenges and the Future of Honors Education

Structural Challenges and the Future of Honors Education

Edited by Robert W. Glover
and Katherine M. O'Flaherty

ROWMAN & LITTLEFIELD
Lanham • Boulder • New York • London

Published by Rowman & Littlefield
A wholly owned subsidiary of The Rowman & Littlefield Publishing Group, Inc.
4501 Forbes Boulevard, Suite 200, Lanham, Maryland 20706
www.rowman.com

Unit A, Whitacre Mews, 26-34 Stannary Street, London SE11 4AB

British Library Cataloguing in Publication Information Available

Library of Congress Cataloging-in-Publication Data Available

ISBN: 978-1-4758-3146-7 (cloth : alk. paper)
ISBN: 978-1-4758-3147-4 (pbk. : alk. paper)
ISBN: 978-1-4758-3148-1 (electronic)

∞ ™ The paper used in this publication meets the minimum requirements of American National Standard for Information Sciences—Permanence of Paper for Printed Library Materials, ANSI/NISO Z39.48-1992.

Printed in the United States of America

Contents

Acknowledgments

The inception for this edited volume and series was an annual meeting of the National Collegiate Honors Council (NCHC) where the editors discussed the growth of honors in higher education and the opportunities and obstacles that such growth might engender in the future. Initially conceived as a single edited volume, the project grew in scope to an edited series as the editors and publisher realized the diverse array of issues that confront anyone aiming to systematically reckon with the complex landscape of honors in higher education. As the title of the series suggests, our current moment is one of transition—motion from the initial stages of growth to a more systematic accounting of what honors education is, and what educators within this field aspire to see it become in the future.

Since that initial kernel of an idea, many individuals have directly or indirectly helped to prod this edited series from fuzzy concept to tangible set of final products. The editors of this volume are extraordinarily grateful to all of the authors in the series who have generously given their time, energy, and expertise. The editors hope that this edited series on teaching and learning in honors will constitute a starting point for a more cohesive, unified, scholarly endeavor. The editors of this volume are deeply grateful to them, and hope that future generations of honors educators, scholars, and students will be as well.

The series editors, Robert W. Glover and Katherine M. O'Flaherty, would like to extend their sincere and deep thanks to Tom Koerner, Vice-President and Editorial Director, and Bethany Janka, Assistant Editor, at Rowman & Littlefield Education. Their editorial vision, commitment to the project, and attention to detail have made this edited series a reality and brought coherence and clarity to the project. Throughout, we have benefitted enormously from working with them and have greatly appreciated their enthusiasm and commitment to the project through all of its stages.

On a personal note, Robert W. Glover would like to thank his enormously supportive friends, colleagues, and family (most especially Nicole Brown; Parker Brown; his mother, Margaret Glover; and his sisters, Carrie and Dianna—all wonderful and important in their own special and unique ways). Katherine M. O'Flaherty would like to thank her colleagues at Barrett, the Honors College at Arizona State University, who continually challenge and shape her thinking about higher education. It is a privilege to work with such a brilliant group of people. She'd also like to thank her wonderful friends near and far; her ever-supportive parents, Patrick and Julia O'Flaherty; and her sister, Patricia O'Flaherty.

Both editors also want to acknowledge and thank their remarkable students, who are the inspiration to consider what we are doing and strive to think about ways in which we might do it better. These talented and highly motivated students are what make honors education possible, but beyond this they make this unique domain of teaching incomparably rewarding, valuable, and fulfilling, both professionally and personally.

Foreword

John Zubizarreta

Much to my bewilderment, I am what I suppose colleagues call a "senior" faculty member because of my tenure in higher education. As with other faculty who thrive on teaching and professional development, I cringe at the label. I am repeatedly asked when I plan to retire, and my response is always the same: Why would I want to leave a profession—more specifically, my twin positions as director of honors and director of faculty development—that I love and that enables me to be creative, experimental, even rogue in both worlds of excellent student learning and engaged teaching?

Honors especially, at its core, encourages and supports the kinds of teaching, learning, scholarship, and service that go beyond the routines of academic endeavors inside and outside the classroom. In this sense, honors challenges existing "structural dynamics in higher education," inviting us to be radical in our philosophies and practices. Honors prompts innovation, the principle that will guide it into a future that is rapidly changing in the landscape of higher education. Such a vision—grounded in practical leading-edge efforts to improve learning, teaching, and the ways in which our institutions do business more broadly—is what gives this volume its coherence and inspiration. Innovation is what keeps me going in honors, and it is a theme that the editors say runs "repeatedly and intentionally" throughout the book's chapters.

Driven as we are by market studies, efficiency measures, calls from outside and inside the academy to produce job-ready workers, strategic plans, outcomes assessment, niche pursuits, competitive advertising, and other quests for the holy grail of being regarded as innovative teachers, scholars, programs, and institutions, we are all pressured to show how we are innovative. But innovation is a squirrelly concept, as the opening chapter in *Structural Challenges and the Future of Honors Education* makes clear. And that is what I admire most about the book.

Instead of pie-in-the-sky claims about how and why honors is magically innovative, the various chapters focus on specific practical ways in which honors makes a difference in student learning, faculty professional growth, and institutional caliber and reputation by providing a stimulating, safe space for learners, teachers, and administrators to venture into new territories, to use the classroom and program design as incubators for new or revised pedagogies, for different program structures, and for continuous change and improvements. Innovation, after all, is more "a product of diligent attention to mundane details, undergirded by a sense of pride and passion" than some unearthly inspiration.

The different authors do not offer up general polemics to combat what the editors describe as significant pushes in higher education today toward corporatization, hegemonic assumptions about the role of technology, and the perceived dichotomy of liberal arts learning versus skills-based preparation for jobs. Instead, each chapter explores and proposes real, tenable, sustainable directions and objectives that may help honors continue to lead in pushing boundaries, fostering creative thinking and action within and without traditional classrooms and institutional structures, and being *innovative*.

Structural Challenges and the Future of Honors Education is both argument and handbook. It identifies particular challenges that continue to mount in higher education and addresses how and why honors must be a key player in the shifting world ahead. It also points the way forward for honors education as an inspiring testing ground for innovations and practical developments in learning, teaching, scholarship, and institutional structures. It contains diverse chapters on structural realities and challenges, connections between honors and gifted education theories, designing seamless transitions from two-year to four-year programs, the power of portfolios in enhancing and assessing honors learning, what honors can learn from Scotland's MA (Hons) system, and how honors can marshal online technologies to adapt to the growing market of online education. It positions honors vitally at the center of the future of higher education. So why would I want to retire?

John Zubizarreta, PhD
Director of Honors and Faculty Development
Carnegie Foundation/CASE U.S. Professor of the Year
Columbia College

Chapter One

Introduction

Confronting Structural Realities and Challenges

Robert W. Glover and Katherine M. O'Flaherty

Though there is a tendency to view science and innovation as identical, a recent conference at the Stevens Institute of Technology focused not on the "innovators" but the "maintainers." The conference assembled "historians, social scientists, artists, activists, and engineers to discuss how the human-built world is maintained and sustained—so often by unnamed, unseen, and underpaid labor."[1] The conference sought to demarcate the two and call attention to the great dangers that accompany privileging innovation at the expense of the basic tasks that enable societal and scientific endeavors to persist.

On the topic of innovation, Scott Berkun states, "the truth is making really good things is difficult—it requires a commitment to craft, an attention to detail, and a love for work that has always been rare. And while we'd never call these three attributes innovations, it's the success of creating an organization that rewards these things that leads to the products we often herald, after they're done, as innovations."[2] In retrospect, we may call the novelties that make modern life so interesting "innovations," but their creation was just as much a product of diligent attention to mundane details, under-girded by a sense of pride and passion.

The conference participants were dealing with broad societal innovations, but honors education can benefit from these insights. Contemporary culture, particularly in higher education, is some-what obsessed with the idea of innovation—of dreaming up some creative vision of the future in the abstract and engaging in the painstaking process of making it a reality. Numerous successive generations have now been told to "think outside the box" (too often in regimented, lifeless settings so thoroughly "inside the box" they could not find their way outside if they tried). But in this hackneyed cliché, there is great cultural symbolism and truth.

From this paradigmatic perspective, thinking within existing structural and cultural parameters almost never yields a bold new vision driven by true *creation* and *innovation*. Only by setting aside these constraints does one create the imaginative space to initiate something that defiantly departs from the past. If the contemporary world has a mantra, it is this quote from the great Jonathan Swift: "vision is the art of seeing things invisible."[3] There is much to be said about this manner of thinking in relation to honors education. The language of innovation has been repeatedly and intentionally used throughout this edited series.

Many, if not most, honors educators structure their courses so as to foster and reward innovative thinking; in fact, this is part of what makes teaching in honors so rewarding and engaging. Furthermore, the proliferation of honors education within colleges and univer-sities can be traced, at least in part, to efforts to cast itself as a thoughtful and creative space that transcends prototypical discipli-nary and pedagogical conventions. It's an intoxicating vision, and one that is not simply disingenuous marketing. Yet this devotion to the cult of innovation can be dangerous.

It can obscure the fact that the structural parameters that one is told to imaginatively "cast off" remain very real, regardless of whatever imaginative conjuring is happening just beyond their reach. In a setting that privileges innovation, it is tempting to forget about these important background conditions. Yet doing so can result in a vision that is untenable, unsustainable, and fails to enmesh within the larger structures where it must eventually reside once translated from innovative vision to day-to-day reality.

Perhaps, in addition to Swift, honors education can take guidance from Karl Marx, who stated, "men make their own history, but they do not make it as they please; they do not make it under self-selected circumstances, but under circumstances existing already, given and transmitted from the past."[4] Marx was referring to larger-scale and often deeply entrenched social and economic realities. But the bottom line is this: innovation happens within larger institutional structures and those structures matter. Any individual or organization has only limited autonomy in relation to these structural constraints.

The first volume in this series largely grappled with the enormous growth in honors education in recent years and the opportunities and challenges it presents for the future. The second volume focused upon curricula and the ways in which honors educators have capitalized on the initial period of growth in honors to fashion distinctive and challenging new pedagogies. This third volume considers how honors might persist in the face of larger structural dynamics in higher education—for instance, the push for online education, calls to demonstrate "return on investment," and market-based pressures to focus attention on specific fields and skills.

THE CHANGING STRUCTURAL LANDSCAPE OF HIGHER EDUCATION

The structural landscape of higher education has changed considerably in recent years, with honors education in many ways representing a counterweight to the larger trends unfolding at universities and colleges in the United States. In this sense, honors education is poised for struggle as it attempts to protect its burgeoning identity in the face of three powerful forces: 1) an increasingly corporatized culture in financial decision making and management, 2) a heightened role for technology-enabled distance learning, and 3) intense debates over the priorities of higher education—generalized, humanistic knowledge versus applied skills and specialization.

Numerous recent critiques have focused on the rise of corporate culture at American institutions of higher education.[5] Among many in academia, there is distaste bordering on disdain for the ways that techniques drawn from corporate boardrooms have found their way into the dominant culture of higher education. Such trends often end up shaping the character of what happens within the classroom. As Stanley Aronowitz writes, "what was once the hidden curriculum—the subordination of higher education to the trends of capital—has become an open policy at public and private institutions."[6]

These critiques are often scathing but compelling, highlighting a number of ubiquitous developments in contemporary higher education: growing cadres of administrators, slick marketing campaigns, increasingly stringent reporting and assessment structures, and budgetary and programmatic decisions being made on the basis of consumer demand rather than holistic educational integrity. Perhaps more troubling is a financial model at many institutions that is so hyper-attentive to generating growth and cutting costs and that relies so heavily on the undercompensated labor of adjunct faculty and graduate students to do the bulk of teaching.

Honors education does not exist in isolation from these trends. From this perspective, honors must justify its own existence, its ability to focus on fewer students and provide them with more resources, while the vast majority of others at their institution attempt to do "more with less." In this setting, honors programs and colleges must also work to fight the perception that they are merely a veneer of rigor and respectability for institutions attempting to churn out as many credit hours as possible for the lowest net cost, existing to "provide prestige for research universities, and also camouflage the failure of their general undergraduate programs."[7]

These developments also impact how those in honors craft a narrative around their endeavor for the purposes of recruitment, development, and program design. If honors students are, from the frame of the dominant paradigm, *consumers* making an investment in their future, then the onus is upon those within honors education to carefully consider "return on investment." What skills are students gaining and how are they poised to succeed as a result? What is the track record of our honors program or college in producing such success? These questions shape and inform any discussion of honors education within the larger college and university structure.

A related structural development is the increasing role of technology-mediated distance education as the platform through which education and pedagogy unfold. According to one recent study, online students had risen to account for 32 percent of total postsecondary degree enrollment by 2011.[8] A more concerning statistic lies in the fact that roughly 35 percent of students enrolled online (over 925,000) were enrolled exclusively in distance education courses at private, for-profit institutions.[9] This industry has been singled out for scrutiny in recent years by the Obama administration for deceptive marketing and predatory financial practices.[10]

Here, too, honors education is impacted and cannot remain oblivious to these larger structural developments. To their credit, honors educators have addressed some of these developments via a forum in the *Journal of the National Collegiate Honors Council* (*JNCHC*) titled "Honors For Sale." Of particular concern, and addressed in a piece by Gary Bell, was a private, for-profit company working to facilitate articulation agreements between community colleges and four-year universities and promising to offer an "honors education," with accompanying academic support and transfer advising, all delivered at least partially online. [11]

To many, the idea of shifting any portion of the honors experience into an online distance education model seems antithetical to what honors purports to offer students. Certainly, if the instrumental value of honors as a recruitment tool for prospective parents and students emphasizes the close bonds between professor and student, that image becomes more difficult to sustain in a distance learning environment. Perhaps for this reason, few within honors have attempted to engage productively with the possibilities of online-mediated distance learning. The immediate goal seems to be critiquing its features deemed most pernicious.

Yet honors education also straddles another important structural challenge related to higher education—a contentious battle over the meaning and character of the educational enterprise itself. At this point, everyone is aware of societal debates over the value of a liberal arts education. This has spawned a cottage industry of articles and opinion pieces defending the broad-based, humanistic, liberal arts approach to education as worthwhile and valuable, with a range of defenses and justifications. [12] There have been so many, in fact, that this led to an op-ed piece about the need for fewer op-eds and more diverse forms of action to defend the liberal arts. [13]

Yet this debate has laid bare a stark cultural disagreement regarding the nature and purpose of education. On the one hand, there are those who view education and the pursuit of knowledge as an intrinsic good, and the ideal form of education as a broadly structured inquiry into the human condition. [14] The purpose of education is not to provide some requisite body of knowledge per se, but to craft and cultivate habits of mind that enable one to be a competent and responsible human.

On the other hand, there are those who see a desperate need for skills and specialization in strategically important areas and see little social value in training individuals who cannot fulfill them. [15]

Edward Conard writes, "If talented workers opt out of valuable training and end up underemployed, not only have they failed to create employment for other less talented workers, they have taken jobs those workers likely could have filled."[16] From this perspective, there is nothing inherently wrong with wanting to study literature or philosophy, but it is viewed as "unallocated talent," likely not producing anything that can provide a broader benefit to society.

This is, of course, a stylized and overgeneralized dichotomy. Between these black-and-white positions are infinite shades of gray. Furthermore, it would be problematic to view honors education as resting firmly in the former perspective and against the latter. There is enormous diversity within honors programs and colleges, many of which center on the acquisition of concrete skills and specializations within one's area of academic study. However, it would not be a stretch to say that the overriding culture of honors education leans toward pedagogies emphasizing interdisciplinary, humanistic liberal arts education.

As a result, honors education finds itself mired in a difference of opinion that is so much more. This debate is part of the contentious cultural confrontations that have gripped our country and on which many partisans can envision no middle ground. Furthermore, it has become a political cause célèbre, informing campaign talking points and leading to troubling policies whereby students not aligning their educational pursuits with current labor market needs should not expect comparable levels of financial aid to those who do.[17] Whether desired or not, much of what is said and done with regard to honors education will be perceived through these lenses.

The larger point is that honors education resides at the fault lines of numerous controversial trends in higher education and society as a whole, and in a challenging proximity to ongoing and contentious debates about the nature of education itself. Any broad conception of what innovative ideas we project into the future cannot ignore these ongoing structural trends. Those within honors education must tread a careful path forward, recognizing the limitations, demands, and perhaps even the opportunities that such structural conditions will create.

CREATIVELY CONFRONTING STRUCTURAL CHALLENGES

The unifying characteristics of the chapters within this volume are that they do not shy away from such challenging structural trends, nor do the scholars and practitioners within this volume set out to merely "critique away" these issues. The tone throughout is one of proactive and productive engagement, encountering these structural dimensions as "interesting problems" to be engaged rather than insurmountable obstacles that must be uniformly critiqued.

In chapter 2, Jaclyn M. Chancey, Jennifer Lease Butts, and Daniel Mercier argue that thus far honors education is not firmly rooted in a theoretical foundation and has not developed new theories of honors education, nor integrated theories from related fields. In this chapter, the authors explore how theoretical frameworks from gifted education and talent development can combine with those from college student development to help practitioners understand honors students and enhance curriculum. This will be an essential task as those within honors education are called upon to more tightly align themselves with larger university visions and structures.

In chapter 3, Brett Nachman examines the challenges faced by community college honors students transitioning to university honors programs. Such students are beset by new challenges in coursework, environment, and goals that might not align with their community college foundations. This chapter focuses on the inconsistencies that plague honors programs in both community colleges and universities and offers suggestions and solutions as to how institutions can implement alternative, more unified methods to assist students in the transfer process.

Chapter 4, by Maureen Kelleher and Lauren Pouchak, focuses on the role and impact of electronic portfolios in facilitating honors academic, advising, and assessment goals. The e-Portfolio is an online system students can use to store materials from their undergraduate experience. Such tools, the authors argue, can provide an evidence-based, accessible documenting of the knowledge, talents, and dispositions gained by students as part of their honors education. Such portfolios align well with goals of systematically tracking what students gain from honors experiences and enabling students to succeed professionally after graduation.

In chapter 5, Darren J. Reid examines what, if anything, can be learned by examining the Scottish MA (Hons) program in place at Scotland's "ancient universities" and applying it to the honors system in the United States. This international focus enables a comparative perspective through which we can examine two forms of education that have broadly aligned goals, but exist in different societal and cultural structures. The chapter examines the impact of the MA (Hons) program in Scotland's education system with an emphasis on what insights this comparative analysis can potentially provide for the future of honors education more generally.

Lastly, in chapter 6, Robert W. Glover and Katherine M. O'Flaherty grapple with the rise of online education and distance learning. As noted earlier, for many the push toward online education is *antithetical* to honors education; the two simply cannot co-exist because to pursue online or hybrid teaching is to undermine or obliterate what makes honors education distinctive and valuable. This chapter attempts to take a less critical and more constructive perspective, utilizing insights from innovations in community engagement and service learning to systematically evaluate the potential roles for online and distance learning in honors education.

Thus while all of these chapters remain carefully attentive to the larger structural features in which honors education is embedded, they retain the core elements of innovation and dynamism that characterize honors education. In this sense, they present a hopeful and constructive vision for the future of honors. Clear-eyed, realist grappling with our future in the face of what can sometimes seem to be troubling systemic trends will propel honors education forward into its next stage of development. The authors represented here all rise to this important challenge.

KEY IDEAS IN THIS CHAPTER

- Innovation in higher education must not occur at the neglect of attention to the structural features and challenges that shape and constrain any such efforts.
- Honors education is not immune from the structural challenges facing higher education more generally, specifically those of the increasingly corporatized culture of university, those related to technology-enabled higher education, and debates over the proper orientation of higher education itself.
- Honors can choose to see these challenges as "interesting problems" that are constructively and proactively confronted, as demonstrated by the chapters included in this volume.

NOTES

1. Laura Bliss, "Innovation Is Overrated," *The Atlantic*, April 11, 2016, accessed May 9, 2016, http://www.theatlantic.com/business/archive/2016/04/innovation-is-overrated/477702/.

2. Scott Berkun, "Why Innovation Is Overrated," *Harvard Business Review*, July 14, 2008, accessed May 9, 2016, https://hbr.org/2008/07/why-innovation-is-overrated.

3. B. D. Colen and Alvin Powell, "The Art of Seeing Things Invisible," *Harvard Gazette*, May 12, 2010, accessed May 9, 2016, http://news.harvard.edu/gazette/story/2010/05/the-art-of-seeing-things-invisible/.

4. Karl Marx, "18th Brumaire of Louis Bonaparte," accessed May 9, 2016, https://www.marxists.org/archive/marx/works/1852/18th-brumaire/ch01.htm.

5. Stanley Aronowitz, *The Knowledge Factory: Dismantling the Corporate University and Creating True Higher Learning* (Boston: Beacon Press, 2000); James E. Côté and Anton Allahar, *Lowering Higher Education: The Rise of Corporate Universities and the Fall of Liberal Education* (Toronto: University of Toronto Press, 2011); Ellen Schrecker, *The Lost Soul of Higher Education: Corporatization, the Assault on Academic Freedom, and the End of the American University* (New York: The New Press, 2013); Gaye Tuchman, *Wannabe U: Inside the Corporate University* (Chicago: University of Chicago Press, 2009); Jennifer Washburn, *University, Inc.: The Corporate Corruption of Higher Education* (New York: Basic Books, 2008).

6. Aronowitz, *The Knowledge Factory*, 81.

7. Murray Sperber, *Beer and Circus: How Big-Time College Sports Has Crippled Undergraduate Education* (New York: Macmillan, 2001), 139.

8. "INFOGRAPHICS: The Growth of Online Education," *The Huffington Post*, accessed April 10, 2016, http://www.huffingtonpost.com/2013/04/12/growth-online-education-moocs_n_3041529.html.

9. Devon Haynie, "New Government Data Sheds Light on Online Learners," *US News and World Report*, June 12, 2014, accessed April 10, 2016, http://www.usnews.com/education/online-education/articles/2014/06/12/new-government-data-sheds-light-on-online-learners.

10. Patricia Cohen, "For-Profit Colleges Accused of Fraud Still Receive U.S. Funds," *The New York Times*, October 12, 2015, accessed April 10, 2016, http://www.nytimes.com/2015/10/13/business/for-profit-colleges-accused-of-fraud-still-receive-us-funds.html.

11. Gary Bell, "The Profit Motive in Honors Education," *Journal of the National Collegiate Honors Council—Online Archive* 15, no. 1 (2014): 12–28.

12. The Council of Independent Colleges (CIC) has a clearinghouse of links to recent pieces in national media defending the liberal arts at http://www.cic.edu/Research-and-Data/Liberal-Arts/Pages/National-Media.aspx.

13. W. Robert Connor, "Higher Ed Needs to Find Better Ways to Make the Case for the Humanities," *Inside Higher Ed*, April 22, 2016, accessed May 1, 2016, https://www.insidehighered.com/views/2016/04/22/higher-ed-needs-find-better-ways-make-case-humanities-essay.

14. Côté and Allahar, *Lowering Higher Education*, 13.

15. Edward Conard, "We Don't Need More Humanities Majors," *Washington Post*, July 30, 2013, https://www.washingtonpost.com/news/innovations/wp/2013/07/30/we-dont-need-more-humanities-majors/.

16. Ibid.

17. Jeffrey Dorfman, "Why Republican Politicians Are Wrong to Push Universities toward Job Training," *Forbes*, accessed May 11, 2016, http://www.forbes.com/sites/jeffreydorfman/2015/03/10/why-republican-politicians-are-wrong-to-push-universities-toward-job-training/#2105f9f53ecf.

Chapter Two

Creating Tomorrow's Honors Education

Theory, Practice, and Student Development

Jaclyn M. Chancey, Jennifer Lease Butts, and Daniel Mercier

A core value in current educational best practices is using research-based theories to inform the manner in which students are educated. An honors education exposes students from a variety of disciplines to a multitude of theoretical perspectives and develops models based on best practices. Yet honors as a profession is not firmly rooted in a theoretical foundation of its own, nor has it systematically integrated theories from related fields. The lack of foundational theories poses challenges to honors administrators as they encounter opportunities and pressures to respond to new educational environments.

There has been important growth in the assessment of honors programs and colleges,[1] but this does not replace the importance of drawing on an appropriate combination of theories when designing and implementing new courses or programs, the success of which can be assessed through program evaluations.[2] Assessment, in turn, is more useful to stakeholders when the theoretical underpinnings of a program's goals, objectives, and activities are incorporated into the evaluation design.[3]

This chapter introduces several theoretical frameworks from gifted education and talent development, college student development, and other useful pedagogy for working with honors students, programming, and curriculum. Several examples refer specifically to the honors program at the University of Connecticut (UConn) and emphasize its incorporation of new instructional technologies and expansion into online space: an immediate challenge for honors education.

GIFTED EDUCATION AND TALENT DEVELOPMENT

Gifted education may elicit images of IQ testing and elementary school pull-out programs irrelevant to the college honors experience. However, the field is much wider, with a variety of theoretical models from which to select, depending on institutional context and program goals. This chapter will focus specifically on talent development frameworks, which describe how to identify and actualize potential for high levels of achievement.

A key tenet of talent development models is that people are talented at *something*. A person's talent exists within a given field and is observable through his or her accomplishments. While some fields, like mathematics, favor early specialization and others, like psychology, tend toward later specialization, the collegiate years generally occupy a place between childhood potential and adult achievement.[4] Honors programs can serve as vehicles through which students first *identify* their talent areas and then further *promote* the development of that talent in preparation for the next stage in their academic, professional, and personal journeys.

Talent Identification

In gifted education literature, a central question is how to identify students who should be served by a given program.[5] Admission remains an important consideration for college honors programs, but this chapter addresses another part of talent identification: finding the field in which an individual will specialize. Honors students declare majors, plan their future education and careers, and excel based on individual patterns of abilities, interests, and values. Honors experiences can help students expand their horizons and then narrow their focuses.

Expanding Horizons

Entering college students tend to have limited views of possible careers and college majors, and there is no evidence that honors students differ in that respect.[6] Thus an important part of talent identification is exposing students to the largest possible cross-section of human endeavors. At some institutions, this may be accomplished in part through general education curricula within or outside of honors.

The work of Joseph Renzulli emphasizes the need for Type 1 enrichment: exposing students to ideas and fields *beyond* what the standard curriculum offers.[7] At UConn, honors students take interdisciplinary honors "Core" courses, which expose them to a greater number of fields as well as some of the ways those fields can interact. Programs may also provide extracurricular Type 1 activities such as visiting speakers, film viewings, or cultural events. Partnerships with other campus departments can increase the number of enriching programs offered to honors students, and the partners in turn benefit from increased event attendance.

The instructors and activity leaders at this stage may be the only representatives of their fields students will meet prior to selecting talent development areas. Effective "first teachers" are enthusiastic, encouraging, and able to communicate why they fell in love with their fields.[8] Too great a focus on rote practice and specific skills at this stage can result in students never developing sufficient interest to commit to such practice.

Activities that are designed to expand honors students' horizons should be evaluated based on their success in generating interest. Do students enroll in the class or attend the event? Does student word of mouth help sustain or build involvement over time? Do students initiate projects or organizations as a result of the activity? Overall, can one observe a diversification of majors over time, from when students enter the university to when they graduate? Finally, do students report that their honors experiences exposed them to new fields or ideas?

Narrowing Focuses

At some point in the talent development process, specialization becomes necessary. While the concept of a "Renaissance person" may be attractive, and there are certainly benefits to being well rounded, few people actually achieve greatness in multiple distinct areas. Some honors students have no problems finding their specialization areas. In fact, some will arrive at college with remarkably specific goals and will likely resist attempts to expand their horizons. However, these students are relatively uncommon.[9]

Far more honors students have some degree of multipotentiality, or "the ability and desire to pursue different activities and goals," due at least in part to admissions practices that favor all-around academic and extracurricular performance.[10] Multipotentiality is not necessarily negative, as these students may enjoy high levels of activity in multiple areas throughout their lives. However, students who are paralyzed by too many choices risk delaying their talent development trajectories.[11] Such delays can place academic and career goals in conflict with personal goals, such as the establishment of a home and family.

There are multiple ways that honors programs can assist students in narrowing their talent development focuses. When students take a wide variety of courses as part of expanding their horizons, they may also identify fields they prefer more than others; additional curricular or extracurricular opportunities within students' fields of interest help them solidify those preferences. [12] At UConn, interdisciplinary honors courses prompt some students to add interdisciplinary majors or minors or to create individualized majors, and discipline-neutral professional advising within honors helps students select or change majors.

Honors students should also be encouraged to consider their extracurricular activities as part of the talent identification process. Early participation in leisure activities—that is, those with limited extrinsic benefits—is a useful predictor of later life choices, including careers. [13] After all, these are activities in which students are developing and applying skills, interests, task commitment, persistence, and other attributes necessary for future talent development. [14] At UConn, honors-sponsored events and multiple honors student organizations provide opportunities for students to specialize outside of the classrooms.

Assessment of honors program efforts in this area may be slightly more difficult than in the previous section. First, students will narrow their focuses at different times and in response to different activities. Second, it is not sufficient to measure when students declare majors. Instead, administrators should look for evidence that students are making concrete future plans. Can they describe something they are passionate about and how they will address it? When do they make postgraduate plans, and can they connect those plans to a larger talent development goal? These are questions that institutional data are unlikely to answer and may require alumni outreach.

Talent Promotion

Talent promotion activities are those that instruct, guide, or encourage an individual in developing his or her talent area.[15] General activities such as fostering helpful social and emotional attributes would be considered talent promotion, as would advanced training within a given discipline. Honors programs and colleges can be places where foundational skills are learned—both general and specific—and where students build upon those skills to become producers of new knowledge.

Social and Emotional Attributes

Every talent development framework includes some acknowledgment of factors other than academic ability or intelligence. For example, Joseph S. Renzulli considers creativity and task commitment to be equally as important as ability.[16] Rena F. Subotnik and colleagues named several psychosocial variables, including motivation, task commitment, and creativity, but did not rank their importance or indicate their list was exhaustive.[17] The list of psychological constructs related to achievement would fill its own volume, so this section is limited to a few key topics specific to gifted education and talent development, plus how these connect to honors practices.

Asynchronous development. Faculty members should beware of assuming that honors students will be equally advanced across multiple academic, social, or personal areas.[18] Gifted students may be further developed than their age peers in one or more academic area while being average or deficient in other academic areas, executive functioning skills, or psychological development.[19] Honors programs should recognize that first-year students who are academically ready for upper-level materials do not necessarily have upper-level self-regulation skills and that honors seniors who are doing graduate-level work are still undergraduates.

Honors students facing these issues may benefit from some Type II enrichment activities,[20] which include any course or activity that explicitly teaches skills needed for advanced productivity, such as project management techniques or teamwork. At UConn, honors students report more successful thesis experiences when they have assistance creating a project plan, multiple check-in points, and supportive faculty mentors who recognize the difference between an undergraduate thesis and a master's or doctoral project.

Intensity. Some honors students demonstrate a kind of intensity in the way they approach their learning, schoolwork, extracurricular activities, and everything else. This fire can be a great force for talent development, but it also brings challenges. For example, intense students may find it difficult to interact appropriately with peers and faculty members who do not share this characteristic, and they may also neglect tasks they see as boring or mundane in favor of more exciting learning opportunities.[21]

Again, these students benefit from honors advisors and mentors who can work with them individually to learn coping skills. UConn Honors promotes frequent opportunities for undergraduate research and experiential learning as productive outlets for this intense drive.

Challenge. Many honors students arrive at college with very little experience dealing with real academic challenge. This may result in poor work and study habits, a lack of study and time management skills, an inability to ask for help, and an entity view of intelligence that sees the need to study as evidence that one is not smart.[22] There is evidence that academically gifted students have more negative physical and emotional reactions to failure.[23]

It is critical that honors programs incorporate real academic challenge and rigor as a way for students to learn task commitment and gain confidence in their own abilities in the face of difficulty. However, it is equally critical that an honors program anticipate the difficulties that students may have when facing challenges for the first time and provide proactive support. At UConn, that support is an explicit consideration when planning many aspects of the honors first-year community—including staffing and peer mentorship programs.

As noted previously, the list of social and emotional attributes that are linked to talent development is virtually endless. Fortunately, many can be measured through simple self-report instruments validated through research with college students, and such instruments could be used in pre/post-testing over a student's honors career.

Advanced Training

For honors students to progress toward expertise and leadership within their chosen talent fields, they must receive advanced training in those fields. At this stage of the talent development process, students have moved beyond the need for the enthusiastic first teacher; instead, they need a supportive expert "second teacher" who will train them in the specific content and methods of the talent area.[24] This may be the same person, as long as he or she can work in both modes and knows when to shift for a given student.

Even when an honors student has little prior knowledge about a field when entering college, he or she is still likely to learn more quickly and in more depth than the standard curriculum offers. Gifted and talented students need responsive curricula that recognize what they already know, what they do not know, what they are ready to learn, and at what pace they need to learn.[25] K–12 teachers use a variety of techniques such as curriculum compacting and telescoping to achieve this goal,[26] but these tend to be less common in postsecondary education.

Like many other programs, UConn allows students and faculty members to enter into honors contracts to modify nonhonors classes to meet the students' needs. The recommendations to faculty are structured to mirror gifted education best practices. UConn honors students also benefit from access to graduate-level courses and a credit overload policy that allows them to register for more than the standard number of courses per semester.

Advanced training does not need to be limited to the classroom, nor should it be limited to academic content. Students in this stage of the talent development process need practice with the real skills they will use in their academic and professional careers such as internships, industry mentorships, and research placements within different disciplines. UConn honors students have honors faculty advisors who can help each student assemble the most appropriate talent development plan.

Some assessment of advanced training efforts can be centralized. This might include assessment of student and alumni perceptions of how well their honors degree programs prepared them for later stages of their academic or professional careers. Institutional data would include information about graduate courses, advanced honors courses, and honors by contract courses taken. However, advanced training is discipline-specific and likely to be delivered within the various academic departments. These partners must be included in the definition of outcomes (how "advanced" training in each area should be) as well as effective and efficient measurement.

Creative Productivity

In most fields, the production of new knowledge or creation of new ideas is the goal. The Subotnik and colleagues model distinguishes between production domains and performance domains (for example, acting).[27] However, the most eminent performers are also those who change the field by doing something new and different.[28] Honors education can be a way for students to move into this stage of their talent development trajectory earlier than normally expected.

Creative productivity is epitomized by Type III activities, in which students apply high levels of ability, creativity, and task commitment to create real products that will be presented to authentic audiences (not just a teacher and classmates).[29] The most obvious example of this in UConn Honors is the honors thesis, but the program also emphasizes a developmental approach to research and innovation, with structured opportunities beginning as early as the first year. This helps students learn necessary skills in supportive environments with their peers.

To fulfill the goals of Type III enrichment, an honors program should provide ways for students to disseminate the results of their work. UConn provides several university-based outlets, including two undergraduate research fairs each year and publication in the same digital commons that hosts faculty and graduate student research. Individual departments also hold research fairs and symposia. Students are further encouraged to present at professional conferences. The number of internal and external publications and presentations can also be used to assess the success of an honors program in promoting creative productivity.

While the field of gifted education and talent development can contribute greatly to understanding honors students, much of this knowledge has been gained through research based in the K–12 school system. Some theorists have begun to explore the psychological experiences of gifted adults,[30] but one must look outside gifted education for frameworks that incorporate the *college* experiences of academically gifted and talented students.

COLLEGE STUDENT DEVELOPMENT THEORY AND HONORS STUDENTS

The period of young adulthood coinciding with the traditional college years is a key time for growth in many developmental theories.[31] Most college student development theories illustrate a collective version of the college student experience, but they generally fail to consider honors students or gifted college students as having separate or distinct experiences. Juxtaposing these theories with those from gifted education, however, does provide a picture of the collegiate life of an honors student and can create better-informed practice.

Developmental Theories and College Students

One of the best comprehensive guides is *Student Development in College: Theory, Research, and Practice.*[32] This work begins with an historical overview of college student development theories and then breaks theories down into three categories: foundational theories, integrative theories, and social identity development. Foundational theories—including Chickering's theory of identity development, Perry's theory of intellectual and ethical development, several moral development theories, and cognitive structural theories—provided the research base from which more recent theories of college student development have emerged.

The integrative theories section includes research that examines the multiple facets of a student's life and the ways in which the college environment might play a role in development. The reader is introduced to ecological theories and the impact of place on college student development, the concept of self-authorship, the role of faith and spirituality in development, and Schlossberg's transition theory as a means of describing the changes a student encounters during the college experience.

The final section turns inward again and examines social identity development. Theories presented include racial identity development, ethnic identity development, multiracial identity development, sexual identity development, and gender and gender identity development. These theories are important reminders that in addition to the intellectual development that should occur as a result of students participating in an honors program, there are many other parts of the self that will also be growing and developing.

Students experience developmental changes in different ways and at different times. A student may be more acutely aware of his or her racial identity once he or she is in the new environment at college; the next semester, however, he or she may be more immersed in understanding the role of gender and his or her gender identity. Honors students experience development growth and changes that are exactly what one would expect from traditionally aged young adults. Understanding a broad base of developmental theories helps prepare honors educators to meet students at their needs.

Schlossberg's Theory of Transition

A specific developmental theory that can be applied to the college student experience for honors students is Schlossberg's Transition Theory.[33] Transitions are defined in this theory as events or nonevents that cause change in a person's life. These can be positive or negative changes, anticipated or unanticipated, and have a profound impact on one's day-to-day life or a small impact. The transition theory offers four areas—the 4 Ss—that shape how a student might handle a transition: situation, self, support, and strategies.

Situation refers to the context in which the transition occurs: the timing, the duration, and the level of control one feels. Self considers demographic characteristics, such as age, gender, race, ethnicity, and socioeconomic status, which contribute to the individual's view of self in the transition. Support measures the means a person has to draw upon resources during the transition, such as familial supports, social supports, or even individual self-supports. Finally, strategies include coping mechanisms and their ability to change the situation, change the way the individual makes meaning of the situation, or manage the stress associated with the situation.

Schlossberg's Transition Theory is integrated into the honors first-year seminar class at UConn because the first semester of college is a period of significant transition in a student's life. Students are living away from home, often for the first time, and are responsible for managing their time, taking care of themselves, and prioritizing tasks and responsibilities. They negotiate new relationships with peers, professors, and staff members on campus while struggling to maintain previous relationships. While many have anticipated going to college for many years, the reality of the situation differs from popular culture's depiction of "college life."

UConn's honors first-year seminar utilizes a team-taught approach, pairing faculty members with peer facilitators to instruct the course. The peer facilitators go through a one-semester training course in which Schlossberg's Transition Theory is among the development theories discussed. They learn about the 4 Ss in order to intervene and assist the first-year students with transitions. Facilitators are trained in the resources available on campus so that they can help provide avenues of *support* for students. Through case studies outlining challenges students face in their first semester, facilitators learn how to help students develop *strategies*.

The course provides an analysis of the first-year experience and information about the diversity of UConn's student body so that facilitators can better understand the roles that *situation* and *self* play in a student's transition to college. The real power of this experience, though, lies in the fact that facilitators also learn better strategies for coping with their own transitions. Facilitators are typically sophomores, and therefore still undergoing acculturation to college.

Utilizing this theory in particular has paid dividends in the ability of UConn Honors to provide peer support to virtually every first-year student in the program. Between fifty and seventy students train to become facilitators each year, creating a cadre of well-informed peers that continue to offer support to students through formal and informal mentoring beyond their time as facilitators. To support an entering class of five hundred honors students, approximately thirty first-year seminar sections are offered, each seating up to nineteen. Even though the course isn't required, approximately 98 percent of first-year students complete the course each year.

Baxter Magolda's Theories of Development

Marcia B. Baxter Magolda calls for educators to do three things to help students develop intellectually: validate students as knowers, situate the learning in the students' experiences, and define learning as a jointly constructed experience.[34] The original research for this theory was based on interviews with 101 college students, beginning in 1986. Subsequent interviews with a large number of participants from the original study resulted in additions to the theory, such as the concept of self-authorship. "Becoming the author of one's own life"[35] is perhaps one of the key tenets of a college education, and it is a phrase often used in honors education as well.

UConn Honors utilizes Baxter Magolda's theories through course development and the promotion of experiential learning for honors students. It is a paradigm shift, to be sure, to go from the all-knowing professor to the professor who explores knowledge with his or her students. It is a shift many honors faculty members have already embraced. One way this is encouraged at UConn is through the interdisciplinary "Core" classes, in which faculty members step outside the comfort of discipline to examine an issue from multiple points of view.

Promoting portfolio assessments, student research presentations in class, and group projects also provides opportunities for students to bring their ideas and experiences into the classroom. The confidence that students gain from these types of educational experiences is critical to their ability to accept the risk and challenge associated with further educational pursuits. The rich learning environment created by infusing this theory into the classroom is also why many UConn honors students and faculty members regard "Core" courses as their favorites to take and to teach.

At UConn, honors students hear about taking ownership of their education early in their college careers, through a variety of opportunities. For example, the "IDEA Grant" program gives students $4,000 to engage in scholarly and creative pursuits based on their own ideas. Past projects include a documentary about Nazi resistance movements, a design for a quad-copter to map locations too dangerous for humans to investigate, and intensive research on invasive plant species. Allowing students to carve out projects that are interesting to them is a critical approach to helping them develop self-authorship in college.

Assessing Honors Student Development

There are a variety of approaches honors staff members can take in assessing development in honors students. One approach would be to survey students using instruments created by college student development researchers. This would provide a snapshot of the program's students, demonstrating potential areas of strength or concern while also highlighting any differences between students in a given honors program and those from the original research.

A longitudinal approach might include pre/post-survey instruments and qualitative, semi-structured interviews with a subset of honors students after each college year. This would yield a rich dataset providing the ability to delve deeply into the ways students have or have not grown and developed in college and what courses, programs, activities, or experiences shaped their development. Rates of retention in and graduation from the honors program can be examined for relationships with activities such as first-year seminar courses or thesis support programs.

Finally, obtaining information from course evaluations can be helpful in understanding the ways in which the structure of a classroom experience shape growth and development in students. The theories discussed in the chapter thus far mainly focus on individual development. The power of an honors program, present or future, lies in the collective experiences of students, and this is perhaps best seen in the curricular structures of honors courses. Examining innovative pedagogies can guide purposeful creation of courses designed for honors student development.

PEDAGOGIES FOR HONORS EDUCATION

Good teaching is purposeful, thoughtful, intentionally designed, and should be grounded in sound theory and proven practice. The effect of new modes of instruction, in particular hybrid and blended learning, will play an increasingly important role in honors education. The terms hybrid and blended can refer to many different learning environments. In this chapter, the terms *hybrid* or *blended* refer to courses in which the percentages of time spent in the physical classroom and outside of the classroom engaged with a learning technology are predetermined. Many of the pedagogies used in hybrid course development complement those used in honors course design.

Learners as Constructors of Knowledge

As stated previously, a significant challenge educators face is the transition students make from high school to university. This includes how to get students to engage with the curriculum as active constructors of knowledge and not as passive recipients of information. Instructors must transition from providing teacher-centered instruction to facilitating student-centered learning to successfully enable and encourage students to become constructors of knowledge. Hybrid and online courses can be great vehicles for engaging learners in this way.[36]

The constructivist approach to course design incorporates authentic, student-centered learning activities and assessments that make use of relevant technologies. In student-centered courses, the instructor's role is that of facilitator as opposed to that of teacher.

Students should be presented with complex problems that allow them to develop interests, knowledge, and skills.[37] These learning experiences should be situated in real-world contexts.[38]

Activities such as field experiences, laboratory work, and community involvement all expose students to authentic learning opportunities, but the traditional classroom, limited resources, and geographic location can make them difficult to incorporate into the curriculum. Online resources developed for hybrid instruction can enable teachers to "expand" or "remove" the four walls of a traditional classroom and provide virtual access to distant experts, far-away places, and resources that would otherwise be unattainable. This provides contextualized activities and tasks that promote student learning.[39]

Online resources can be used to address many limitations of the physical classroom. For instance, one film studies course at UConn required that students review and critique films and later present a paper comparing and contrasting them. The films were always in limited supply. The instructor expressed concern that it had become difficult to deliver this course without using class time to view the films, and he also felt that the final papers did not adequately assess the student learning outcomes identified for the course.

In the redesigned course, streaming media allowed students greater access to movies and films online, and thus more time to interact during class. The final paper was replaced with themed virtual film festivals authored using a content management system. Multimedia constructions such as this represent active learning, promote deep formulation of knowledge, and allow instructors to observe students' learning processes.[40] Many in-person honors courses could be enhanced through similar additions of online components or multimedia student products.

Keller's Motivational Design Model

Maintaining student motivation can be a difficult task in a traditional learning environment, despite the fact that there has been a great deal of research in that area. To date, there has been less research into the effects of motivation on students taking online or blended courses, but there is evidence that student motivation can be influenced by course design. In order to maintain motivation throughout a course, one must stimulate curiosity, certify relevance, appropriately challenge students, and provide positive outcomes. [41]

John M. Keller's ARCS model is often used to address and maintain these elements while designing learning activities. [42] The process begins by designing activities that gain the learner's interest, or *attention*. Activities are made *relevant* to the learner through connections to their goals, learning styles, and past experiences. [43] Learner *confidence* is increased when students "experience success under conditions where they attribute their successes to their own abilities and efforts rather than to luck or the task being too easy or difficult." [44] Finally, learner *satisfaction* occurs when students have "positive feelings about their learning experiences." [45]

This model can be applied to the development of hybrid courses using case studies. Cases are designed to challenge the learner by presenting interesting, unresolved problems specific to the discipline in question. Developed using the same constructivist approach described earlier, the scenarios are as authentic as possible, requiring learners to apply past knowledge and experience to typical scenarios one might encounter in the professional workplace.

Courses designed in this manner utilize the face-to-face portion of the course to provide initial information regarding the case as well as feedback and clarification along the way. Much of the students' interaction with the case happens in the asynchronous, online portion of the course, with the instructor as "guide on the side" providing prompt feedback and encouragement. Student deliverables and assessments may include items such as marketing plans, press releases, holistic animal care plans, or other portfolio-based forms of assessment.

Case studies can be integrated into honors classes across the talent development trajectory, as they are likely to generate interest in introductory courses and can also be effective vehicles for advanced skill training. Case-based instruction also lends itself well to interdisciplinary courses. Faculty members from participating disciplines contribute their individual expertise and perspectives to the case, thus creating a richer, more authentic learning experience. Students may then be asked to approach the problem from multiple perspectives, allowing for deeper appreciation of the subject matter.

CONCLUSION

Honors education has yet to establish a clear theoretical foundation on which to build programs. A scholarly approach to administration must incorporate theories in the decision-making process; program evaluation and assessment help determine whether those decisions are correct and applied appropriately. Honors is stronger if viewed as an interdisciplinary field emerging from established fields, such as gifted education, college student development, and pedagogy, while simultaneously creating unique scholarship on its own.

Although presented individually, theoretical frameworks such as those detailed in this chapter are easily integrated in practice. For example, UConn Honors offers grants for faculty developing new, innovative first- and second-year honors courses (some of which will also be modified for addition to the regular curriculum after piloting in honors). Course development proposals are evaluated for student-centered pedagogy that promotes increased ownership of education, appropriate levels of academic challenge, and the ability to generate student interest in previously unexplored fields.

Theory allows for the same criteria to be applied to proposals for online or hybrid courses, as these goals transcend course delivery method. Theory also supports additional differentiation and the establishment of specific criteria for third- or fourth-year honors students working within their majors. Creating tomorrow's honors education will require responding to unforeseen changes in students, technology, and the overall landscape of higher education. Strong theoretical foundations can support agile decision making without a loss of professional identity.

KEY IDEAS IN THIS CHAPTER

- Though honors education has grown at an enormous pace, no corresponding development of theoretical foundations to support honors pedagogy has emerged alongside it.
- This is a noteworthy gap, as coherent scholarship of teaching and learning and pedagogical practice will depend upon a shared conceptual foundation in this approach to learning.
- Theoretical frameworks from gifted education and talent development, college student development, and other areas of research and practice are offered here as a useful means by which honors educators can guide their efforts at student advising, programming, and curriculum.
- This chapter also introduces learning theories and models of pedagogical practice for working with honors students, honors programming, and curriculum construction.

NOTES

1. Gregory W. Lanier, "Towards Reliable Honors Assessment," *Journal of the National Collegiate Honors Council* 9, no. 1 (2008): 81–116.

2. For more detail, see Knefelkamp's practice-to-theory-to-practice (PTP) model in Nancy J. Evans et al., *Student Development in College: Theory, Research, and Practice*, second edition (San Francisco, CA: Jossey Bass, 2010), 353–54.

3. Huey-Tsyh Chen, "The Conceptual Framework of the Theory-Driven Perspective," *Evaluation and Program Planning* 12, no. 4 (1989): 391–96.

4. Rena F. Subotnik, Paula Olszewski-Kubilius, and Frank C. Worrell, "Rethinking Giftedness and Gifted Education: A Proposed Direction Forward Based on Psychological Science," *Psychological Science in the Public Interest* 12, no. 1 (2011): 32.

5. Joseph S. Renzulli, ed., *Identification of Students for Gifted and Talented Programs*, Essential Readings in Gifted Education (Thousand Oaks, CA: Corwin Press, 2004).

6. Meredith J. Greene, "Helping Build Lives: Career and Life Development of Gifted and Talented Students," *Professional School Counseling* 10, no. 1 (2006): 34–42; Barbara A. Kerr and Nicholas Colangelo, "The College Plans of Academically Talented Students," *Journal of Counseling and Development* 67 (1988): 42–48.

7. Joseph S. Renzulli, "The Enrichment Triad Model: A Guide for Developing Defensible Programs for the Gifted and Talented," *Gifted Child Quarterly* 20, no. 3 (1976): 317–26.

8. Benjamin S. Bloom, "The Master Teachers," *Phi Delta Kappan* 63, no. 10 (1982): 664; Joseph S. Renzulli, "A General Theory for the Development of Creative Productivity through the Pursuit of Ideal Acts of Learning," *Gifted Child Quarterly* 36, no. 4 (1992): 180–81.

9. Greene, "Helping Build Lives," 36–37; for practical information about the challenges facing such "early emergers," see Bonnie C. Marshall, "Career Decision Making Patterns of Gifted and Talented Adolescents: Implications for Career Education," *Journal of Career Education* 7, no. 4 (1981): 307–8.

10. Seyed Hossein Sajjadi, F. Gillian Rejskind, and Bruce M. Shore, "Is Multipotentiality a Problem or Not? A New Look at the Data," *High Ability Studies* 12, no. 1 (2001): 30.

11. Kathy J. Rysiew, Bruce M. Shore, and Rebecca T. Leeb, "Multipotentiality, Giftedness, and Career Choice: A Review," *Journal of Counseling and Development* 77, no. 4 (1999): 423–30.

12. Sajjadi, Rejskind, and Shore, "Is Multipotentiality a Problem?"

13. Rysiew, Shore, and Leeb, "Multipotentiality, Giftedness, and Career Choice."

14. Eunsook Hong, Susan C. Whiston, and Roberta M. Milgram, "Leisure Activities in Career Guidance for Gifted and Talented Adolescents: A Validation Study of the Tel-Aviv Activities Inventory," *Gifted Child Quarterly* 37, no. 2 (1993): 65–68.

15. Subotnik, Olszewski-Kubilius, and Worrell, "Rethinking Giftedness."

16. Joseph S. Renzulli, "The Three-Ring Conception of Giftedness: A Developmental Model for Promoting Creative Productivity," in *Conceptions of Giftedness*, ed. Robert J. Sternberg and Janet E. Davidson, second edition (New York: Cambridge University Press, 2005), 256–66.

17. Subotnik, Olszewski-Kubilius, and Worrell, "Rethinking Giftedness."

18. Janis K. Guerrero and Shelley A. Riggs, "The Preparation and Performance of Freshmen in University Honors Programs: A Faculty Perspective," *Journal of Secondary Gifted Education* 8 (1996): 41–48; Paul F. Haas, "Honors

Programs: Applying the Reflective Judgment Model," *Liberal Education* 78 (1992): 20–23.

19. Linda Kreger Silverman, "The Construct of Asynchronous Development," *Peabody Journal of Education* 72, nos. 3–4 (1997): 36–58.

20. Joseph S. Renzulli, "The Enrichment Triad Model: A Plan for Developing Defensible Programs for the Gifted and Talented," *Gifted Child Quarterly* 21, no. 2 (1977): 228–32.

21. Rena B. Lewis, Margie K. Kitano, and Eleanor W. Lynch, "Psychological Intensities in Gifted Adults," *Roeper Review* 15, no. 1 (1992): 25–31.

22. Nancy M. Robinson, "The Role of Universities and Colleges in Educating Gifted Undergraduates," *Peabody Journal of Education* 72, nos. 3–4 (1997): 217–19.

23. Shawn M. Roberts and Suzanne B. Lovett, "Examining the 'F' in Gifted: Academically Gifted Adolescents' Physiological and Affective Responses to Scholastic Failure," *Journal for the Education of the Gifted* 17, no. 3 (1994): 241–59.

24. Bloom, "Master Teachers," 664–65.

25. Matthew C. Makel, Martha Putallaz, and Jonathan Wai, "Teach Students What They Don't Know but Are Ready to Learn: A Commentary on 'Rethinking Giftedness and Gifted Education,'" *Gifted Child Quarterly* 56, no. 4 (2012): 198–201.

26. Nicholas Colangelo, Susan G. Assouline, and Miraca U. M. Gross, *A Nation Deceived: How Schools Hold Back America's Brightest Students*, vol. 1 (Iowa City: University of Iowa, 2004).

27. Rena F. Subotnik, Paula Olszewski-Kubilius, and Frank C. Worrell, "Rethinking Giftedness and Gifted Education: A Proposed Direction Forward Based on Psychological Science," *Psychological Science in the Public Interest* 12, no. 1 (2011): 32.

28. Subotnik, Olszewski-Kubilius, and Worrell, "Rethinking Giftedness," 30–32; Rena F. Subotnik and Linda Jarvin, "Beyond Expertise: Conceptions of Giftedness as Great Performance," in *Conceptions of Giftedness*, ed. Robert J. Sternberg and Janet E. Davidson, second edition (New York: Cambridge University Press, 2005), 343–57.

29. Renzulli, "Enrichment Triad Model: A Plan," 232–33.

30. For example, see Stephanie Tolan, "Discovering the Gifted Ex-Child," *Roeper Review* 17, no. 2 (1994): 134–38.

31. For example, see Marcia B. Baxter Magolda, *Knowing and Reasoning in College: Gender-Related Patterns in Students' Intellectual Development* (San Francisco, CA: Jossey-Bass, 1992); Arthur W. Chickering and Linda Reisser, *Education and Identity*, second edition (San Francisco, CA: Jossey-Bass, 1993); and Erik H. Erikson, *Childhood and Society*, second edition (New York: Norton, 1964).

32. Evans et al., *Student Development in College*.

33. Jane Goodman, Nancy K. Schlossberg, and Mary L. Anderson, *Counseling Adults in Transition: Linking Practice with Theory*, third edition (New York: Springer, 2006).

34. Baxter Magolda, *Knowing and Reasoning in College*.

35. Marcia B. Baxter Magolda, *Making Their Own Way: Narratives for Transforming Higher Education to Promote Self-Development* (Sterling, VA: Stylus, 2001), xix.

36. Jay Caulfield, *How to Design and Teach a Hybrid Course: Achieving Student-Centered Learning through Blended Classroom, Online, and Experiential Activities* (Sterling, VA: Stylus, 2011).

37. Curtis Jay Bonk and Donald J. Cunningham, "Searching for Learner-Centered, Constructivist, and Sociocultural Components of Collaborative Educational Learning Tools," in *Electronic Collaborators: Learner-Centered Technologies for Literacy, Apprenticeship, and Discourse*, ed. Curtis Jay Bonk and Kira S. King (Mahwah, NJ: Lawrence Erlbaum Associates, 1998), 25–50.

38. John Seely Brown, Allan Collins, and Paul Duguid, "Situated Cognition and the Culture of Learning," *Educational Researcher* 18, no. 1 (1989): 32–42.

39. Jan Herrington, Ron Oliver, and Thomas C. Reeves, "Patterns of Engagement in Authentic Online Learning Environments," *Australian Journal of Educational Technology* 19, no. 1 (2003): 59–71.

40. Badrul H. Khan, ed., *Web-Based Instruction* (Englewood Cliffs, NJ: Educational Technology Publications, 1997).

41. Ibid.

42. John M. Keller, "The Systematic Process of Motivational Design," *Performance and Instruction* 26, no. 9–10 (1987): 1–8.

43. John M. Keller and Katsuaki Suzuki, "Learner Motivation and E-Learning Design, A Multinationally Validated Process," *Journal of Educational Media* 29, no. 3 (2004): 231.

44. Weiner, cited in ibid.

45. Ibid.

Chapter Three

Bridging the Academic Gap

Brett Nachman

It is a mistake to think honors education only exists at the four-year university. Programs at hundreds of community colleges throughout the United States offer additional educational resources and opportunities to students not enrolled at universities. The goals of these community college honors programs differ from university-level honors programs, in that community colleges focus on a diverse range of students with somewhat different educational and career goals. The universal end goal is the same: to enlighten the minds of scholarly individuals and to provide "a workshop for educational experimentation."[1]

Honors students depart their community college ponds and enter a sea of uncertainty upon entering honors colleges and programs at four-year institutions. This transition marks an imitable period of time, one in which students may be presented challenges, asked to transition into a new system, or one in which they feel like they may drown in open waters with no assistance. Because the purpose behind honors education is to "recruit and serve high achieving students who might otherwise go elsewhere,"[2] honors students essentially exist in innovative environments in which they are provided tools to apply concepts across various disciplines and mediums.[3]

Community college honors programs operate with the goal of motivating hard-working students and training them for the demands of an honors program or college at the university level.[4] Yet gaps exist that lead some of these high-achieving students entering four-year programs to feeling unprepared and overwhelmed with more taxing content and different expectations at the university level.

The discomfort stems from a lack of uniformity in how community college honors programs and university honors programs or colleges design their objectives for students. Honors education primes students not only to be more critical of the world around them, but also to challenge their perceptions. Sadly, the inconsistencies and lack of communication that plague relationships between two-year and four-year institutions may unintentionally inhibit transfer students' development and progress. Honors education within higher education cannot sustain this trend of ignoring these populations, for they will further alienate students and reduce student success.

It is essential to explore why institutional rationales at both the community college and four-year university level have not centered more on collaborating in the development of honors. The general lack of literature that exists on this topic highlights the issue, thus this chapter aims to explore how community college honors programs can align with honors at universities. The chapter also echoes arguments made in other chapters in this series concerning how honors might become more accessible to a wider diversity of students.

Institutional leaders must shape paths for current and future community college honors transfer students, in order for these students not to feel adrift in an ocean without direction. Identifying how to improve connections, making the transition process for honors students smoother, more explicit, and supported, will enable educators to reform their honors programs and increase the retention and success of transfer students. Strengthening ties and understanding how community college honors programs factor into the overall picture will enable more informed policy.

HISTORY

While community college honors programs are not new, they have grown in popularity in recent years. In the 1970s, universities experienced low incoming transfer student rates, which correlated with the dissolution of many community college honors programs. Part of the problem was that many universities were not admitting community college transfer students because they were not academically prepared to handle upper-division work.[5]

By the end of the decade, more community colleges started focusing not only on enabling access for a wider group of individuals (coming from more disadvantaged economic backgrounds), but also ensuring that these institutions possessed academic quality.[6] In the 1980s, researchers began evaluating the place of students seeking academic achievement in community college environments, which often lacked those opportunities. "Higher ability students were entering community colleges because of convenience and rising costs at four-year institutions, and more mature learners were returning to school for various reasons."[7]

This prompted many community colleges to experiment with honors programs for the first time or, in some cases, reintroduce honors programs that had previously folded. "The proliferation of programs targeted to specialized student populations may be indicative of broader organizational and structural changes in the community colleges brought about by instabilities in funding and student composition."[8]

A recent *Peterson's* article suggests that currently more than one-third of two-year (community) colleges offer honors programs.[9] In 2000, David Baker, Sean Reardon, and Kate Riordan

observed that more than 40 percent of community colleges offer
honors programs and colleges.[10] Likewise, 36 percent of the community colleges Charles L. Outcalt analyzed had honors programs,
though he warned that the data was not representative, especially
because he was unable to determine geographical similarities.[11]

By contrast, Bridget T. Long references Barron's *Profiles of
American Colleges* to claim that, as of the early 2000s, only 6.5
percent of community colleges offer honors programs.[12] The level
of discrepancy is startling and speaks to inherent issues in community college honors programs: many are simply overlooked when
counting institutions with honors programs. The aforementioned
scholars are among the few exposing the lack of scholarship on
community college honors programs.

THE COMMUNITY COLLEGE HONORS PROGRAM

What characterizes a community college honors program? This
question seems hard to answer, considering the variety of missions
of individual colleges, districts, and states. However, some key
characteristics demonstrate their similarities to and uniqueness
from four-year institutions' honors programs.

Much like their four-year institutional counterparts, community
college honors programs aim to build institutional status and draw
in high-performing students through their academic programming.[13] Additionally, community college honors programs hope to
retain these students.[14] Considering that community colleges cope
with retention issues, it could be argued that the task is exacerbated
for their honors programs, which may compete with four-year institutional schools for drawing such an appealing student population.

Yet perhaps what makes community college honors programs
most distinct is their necessity to train academically capable students to feel ready for coursework and opportunities at four-year
institutions where they may transfer.[15] Outcalt argued that a major

issue with literature focusing on community college honors programs has been the dearth of attention on composite characteristics among several programs, as scholars tend to solely center on specific traits of individual programs.[16]

On the other hand, some contend that honors programs at community colleges may not be suitable, considering these institutions often serve remedial students.[17] Because many community college students may only seek job training, honors education may not serve a purpose for a sizable student population.[18] The point of community colleges having honors programs then comes into question. However, these programs give students a platform to explore the interdisciplinary nature of courses and extracurricular activities, which can be viewed as worthwhile.

Jeffrey Berger noted that interdisciplinary humanities courses offered in many programs centered on courses with thorough analytical thinking, reading, and writing.[19] For example, San Diego Community College District's (SDCCD) honors programs created courses with more depth and rigor, incorporating relationships among many disciplines and incorporating innovative teaching and learning approaches.[20]

SDCCD also encourages incorporating leadership experience in honors classes, whether students facilitate classroom dialogues or conduct study groups.[21] Honors students take interdisciplinary classes, which compel them to demonstrate knowledge among a diverse set of subjects. These courses not only broaden students' thinking, but are also linked to four-year institutional coursework, thus setting students up for success and easing the transfer process.[22]

A number of researchers have observed that community college honors programs build critical thinking skills through conveying academic content in a more complex manner than traditional coursework. Joseph P. Byrne suggested that these programs' intentions are to produce citizens who find meaningful connections in different areas of their lives.[23] In this way, community college honors programs may inspire students, especially from disadvantaged neighborhoods, to stimulate dialogue and change in their communities, through utilizing the knowledge attained from their coursework.

Berger argued that Community College of Philadelphia's honors program constructed an intellectual atmosphere with classes featuring more opportunities for discussions.[24] Accordingly, Greg Phillips argued that community college honors programs increase classroom participation[25] and Herald R. Kane noted that honors courses encourage students to use more academic sources, create more meaningful papers and presentations, and take advantage of community service and leadership opportunities.[26]

The extracurricular aspect of these honors programs is often tied to participation in service learning opportunities and student organizations like Phi Theta Kappa (PTK) Honor Society chapters. Honors students from San Diego City College said they most enjoyed the academic, social, and cultural events outside of the classroom, as well as engaging in its PTK chapter. These outlets allowed students to build trust and connections with each other.[27]

Each of these factors accounts for successful honors programs and illustrates the depth of honors programs at community colleges. Community colleges are uniquely positioned to offer robust learning opportunities to honors students whether or not those students plan to transfer to four-year institutions. Yet as noted earlier, community colleges and community college transfer students face a range of challenges.

CHALLENGES

Community college honors programs are not immune from the problems that plague community colleges in general. For one, faculty and administrators of community college honors programs must realize that their honors students differ from those at the university level. For example, Berger observed in his research that liberal arts honors program students at community colleges consistently did not attend classes or, at the very least, showed up late.[28] "A successful honors program, therefore, has to be organized to block these behaviors and to encourage a rigorous attitude towards studies that will serve students well when they transfer to other colleges."[29]

Berger suggests that some honors transfer students struggle when they arrive at the university because they simply lack the academic discipline necessary to succeed. Part of the problem may be that honors programs, no matter the institutional level, are too lenient in the students they accept, focusing more on academic performance over student ability to adapt to the new academic environment.[30]

These community college honors students often have drastically different lives compared to their university peers. Many students are older, possess family responsibilities, and live farther from campus than traditional college freshmen. Some community college honors students may return to higher education after several years, making them inherently dissimilar from students transitioning directly from high school.

Some university-level program coordinators and faculty fail to appreciate these unique characteristics. This could be a factor in why there is so much disparity between honors students at various levels, as expectations of these types of students greatly differ. Recent studies have shown that about one-third of community college students are caring for family members, indicating that they possess many commitments outside of school.[31]

A 2012 Community College Survey of Student Engagement determined that "42% of part-time students and 19% of full-time students attending community colleges work more than 30 hours per week."[32] Community college students who are enrolled in school part-time and attend intermittently were less likely to complete their degrees.[33] Attrition rates often run higher than some might want to digest according to Jeffrey G. Garrison, who cited a few studies from the early 2000s that found fewer than 25 percent of honors program students ended up completing them.[34] Clearly, competing obligations undergird these student populations from remaining in college in many cases.

Community college honors programs, as well as honors colleges at universities, can reduce this concerning decline by establishing measures that more consistently track student progress, intervening before these students reach the tipping point of disillusionment and dismay. Much like mediating at-risk youth, honors administrators, staff, and faculty are vital in recognizing students in jeopardy of dropping out and offering resources. Enhanced honors education should place more emphasis on following student progress.

Sometimes, though, honors faculty experience more frustration than the disgruntled honors students. Jeffrey Berger noted that one of the problems with maintaining cohesion in any honors program is the issue of faculty members creating their own approaches to classes and disagreeing over what constitutes an honors experience. Uncompromising faculty members tend to drop out of teaching honors courses, but in turn, incorporating innovative pedagogical tools may enhance faculty members' likelihood of remaining to teach in honors programs.[35]

Floyd and Holloway noted that these programs might inadvertently create faculty hierarchies.[36] While some institutions, such as Oklahoma State University's honors colleges, have allowed adjunct faculty to teach "lower-division Honors courses," save for special circumstances, administrators limit these educators from lecturing in front of honors students.[37]

Not much research has been conducted on adjunct faculty teaching honors courses, but perhaps programs allowing this practice exist in limited number. Instead, students are assigned to more "experienced" faculty, considered more qualified than their adjunct counterparts because of their full-time status. Though these findings may not be representative, they pinpoint an issue intrinsic in any academic environment: contrasting opinions among educators and disdain toward those lower on the faculty food chain.

ELITISM

Some individuals take umbrage with the existence of community college honors programs, believing that they promote elitism, entirely paradoxical to the mission of open-access community colleges.[38] Various "critics assert that such selective programming has no place" in these types of institutions.[39] Robert D. Bolge argued that universities in general have expanded their populations over the decades, increasing access for women, African Americans, nontraditional-aged students, and international students to partake in educational institutions. Until recent years these populations had not enrolled in significant numbers.[40]

Faculty opposed to the honors program at the College of Lake County in Illinois argued that this type of program encouraged segregation. They pointed out that many honors students were not representative of the community college body, which encompassed students of different age, economic, and racial backgrounds.[41]

Moreover, Garrison noted that white females account for the majority of participants in community college honors programs.[42] Specific percentages across programs nationwide are challenging to identify. However, San Jacinto College in Texas, for instance, has an honors program that featured a 6:4 ratio of female to male students in its honors program.[43]

Some colleges work to diversify their student populations. San Diego Community College District aimed to reduce perceptions of elitism in promotional efforts by using the tagline "Excellence with Access," which emphasized representativeness.[44] Meanwhile, Itawamba Community College in Mississippi has incorporated content related to experiences of underrepresented minorities into the honors program curriculum.[45]

"Because the word *honors* itself seemed to be a lightning rod, several programs were driven to use new titles and acronyms for their programs, to finesse the volatile issues of favoritism or elitism that had proven to be endemic to the development of honors programs across the country."[46] Using *transfer* and *scholar* in titles can avoid elitist sentiments while reinforcing the objectives behind these programs at community colleges.[47] As for university-level honors colleges, more neutral language, such as implementing "Academic Institute," might diminish perceptions of exclusivity.

Greg Phillips suggested that community college honors programs lowering admission requirements could reduce perceived elitism, thereby allowing more students to gain program benefits.[48] Should GPA and educational background serve as the main factors for admission? These do not give a full picture of a student's potential. Those who demonstrate a passion to commit to this venture should be granted that opportunity, at the very least for a trial period.

Honors program administrators can evaluate the results (for instance, by determining if students' grades are stable and if they have shown to contribute to the honors program) and make the call if these students can remain or not. Perhaps an experiment akin to this would prove fruitful in reducing the disparity that separates honors students from nonhonors college students.

Community colleges sometimes consider their honors programs to be "crown jewels." If the honors programs lower the admissions criteria, this might reduce prestige and quality. Consequently, this may make it more difficult for community college honors programs' students to transition to university-level honors programs or colleges. This could explain, in part, why some institutions may not communicate with one another about their standards and structures.

But articulation agreements can reduce these issues to an extent. Prince George Community College in Maryland, like some other community college honors programs, uses articulation agreements with a handful of universities to guarantee honors credits to transfer students.[49] "In addition to relieving stress and diminishing uncertainty, clear codified articulation agreements guarantee shorter time to graduation for transfer students," although this fails to explain how the articulation agreement is a "guarantee."[50]

Yet many students belong to institutions where articulation agreements are nonexistent. Students suffer in an environment of turbulent or absent relationships between community college honors programs and university-level honors programs and colleges. Studies, such as Charles L. Outcalt's research from the late 1990s, demonstrate that some community college honors programs do not serve the diverse students attending community colleges.[51]

Outcalt advocated for a large-scale study exploring the role of community college honors programs in predicting student success and determining if they promoted elitism.[52] He evaluated data from a previous study by the Center for the Study of Community Colleges, analyzing institutional, curriculum, and student characteristics from 163 community colleges' catalogues.[53]

He found that community college honors programs were more prevalent in schools with a higher percentage (constituting more than 40 percent of the student body) of Latino students. Nevertheless, Outcalt warned that the community colleges featured in the study were not representative of all similar types of institutions in the United States and that there may not be causality.[54] Community colleges offering honors programs had an African American enrollment rate of less than 3 percent.[55]

Outcalt performed linear regression to look at these relationships more closely and argued that "people who are committed to equity within the educational opportunities available to African Americans have reason to be concerned by these findings."[56] He suggested that while these findings suggest elitism to some extent, "these conclusions must remain tentative pending further investigation of actual enrollment and success in honors programs according to student characteristics."[57]

Sadly, the results perpetuate the belief that community college honors programs are elitist. At the very least, the discoveries point to a low percentage of African American community college students participating in these honors programs. Though the studies described in this chapter did not clearly identify a single factor for why minority students may not enroll in honors programs, perceived elitism and lack of promoting honors to diverse audiences may dissuade some academically capable students from applying.

More research must be conducted to determine if these enrollment trends among underrepresented students in community college honors programs are systematic nationwide. Likewise, community college honors programs must implement substantial measures related to advocating accessibility and content development, akin to what San Diego and Itawamba have accomplished.

COMMUNITY COLLEGE AND UNIVERSITY PARTNERSHIPS

Community college honors programs possess the potential to thrive and produce well-prepared students transitioning to four-year institutions. However, much of this success is contingent on partnerships forged between community college honors programs and university-level honors programs or colleges. Some community college honors programs produce smart and competent students, but students may lack the guidance and preparedness to transition because of few connections in place between community college honors programs and university-level honors programs or colleges.

It is essential for partnerships to exist between institutions in order for these honors transfer students to effectively integrate into their new academic environments. Several case studies of various colleges and institutions building rapports and starting initiatives to support these students illustrate simple yet substantial resources that can bolster honors education and serve as a template for future honors partnerships.

Florida's Miami Dade College is a leading example of how organizing resources and building bonds can help community college honors students, especially traditionally underrepresented populations. Miami Dade, consisting of several campuses, consolidated its honors program in 2001 to make content more consistent. Its program, consisting of various opportunities, including academic conferences and internships, speaks to the breadth of opportunities typically available only at the university level.[58]

Additionally, all Miami Dade honors students earn a scholarship award that covers tuition, books, and a stipend.[59] What makes the honors program unique, outside of the partnership that guarantees honors graduates receive full tuition to Florida International University and admittance into Honors College, is the fact that approximately 73 percent of Miami Dade's honors students are Hispanic.[60] As 68 percent of honors students are female, this echoes similar demographic trends noted earlier at San Jacinto College.[61]

"Critics who believe that honors programs are not egalitarian should note that Miami Dade's program serves a diverse clientele of students."[62] The substantial honors program gives students the chance to attend lectures, partake in rigorous interdisciplinary courses, serve the community, and earn at least thirty-six credits in honors courses to graduate.[63]

Perhaps Miami Dade's intensive and extensive honors program, complemented by its relationship with Florida International, sets its students up well for future academic endeavors. In fact, some of its honors alumni end up transferring to and graduating from many prestigious institutions, including Columbia, Yale, Stanford, Northwestern, and the University of Wisconsin–Madison.[64]

Likewise, Santa Monica College in California has a "Scholars Program" that possesses many benefits, including "priority admissions consideration to University of California, Los Angeles, and several other universities, along with special counseling, workshops, priority registration, smaller class sizes, and special college tours."[65]

California possesses a long history in developing partnerships between community colleges and its two public four-year institutions, but transfer students still account for a much lower proportion of new students compared to freshmen.[66] The state made community colleges more of a priority following an economic recession that prompted individuals to believe more underrepresented students would enroll in these institutions.[67]

A 1997 "Memorandum of Understanding" involved the University of California's (UC) lofty goal of raising enrollment of students from community colleges by around 50 percent by the end of the 2005–2006 academic year. Furthermore, the University of California, often considered selective in student intake, said it would be more open in enrolling more students lacking a traditional educational background.[68]

While this effort encompassed all community college students—not necessarily just honors students—its development and success reflect the opportunities that could be translated to community college honors programs specifically. The community colleges incorporated more counselors and transfer specialists who met with students to discuss transitioning to University of California (UC) schools, as well as formed more articulation agreements to ensure credits would transfer.[69]

These arrangements are intended to prevent students from repeating similar courses, in addition to ensuring that students feel more academically prepared for university-level courses.[70] In this example, the structures aligned with one another, leading students to flourish. Over the eight-year period, UC enrolled about 33 percent more transfer students, even within its more competitive campuses like UCLA.[71]

Additionally, schools, like those under the University of California's umbrella, have been communicating clear messages to transfer students that indicate these students are academically capable of succeeding. Many of these community college students have been stereotyped as not being competitive with their university-level peers. Students with lower socioeconomic status also worry about the financial feasibility of advancing in their education at the university level.[72]

If universities focus more on educating these transfer students about the transition to those institutions and offer programs to help them based on their life situations, community college students may reconsider enrolling in universities.[73] Likely, if honors colleges at universities adopt a similar approach with community college honors students, they may experience increased admittance rates and higher confidence from those who apply.

The research also focused on the importance of forming a "transfer-going culture" that sets up students—who begin their college experiences at community college—for success.[74] This can be extended to honors students at community colleges if coordinators from the university-level honors college are brought in to establish those relationships.

"UC campuses that have been successful in attracting and graduating transfer students have developed initiatives such as transfer-orientation programs, transfer centers . . . and transfer-themed housing options."[75] It could be assumed that these would also work for honors students if they were provided with the same amenities, but the structure must first be in place.

Another beneficial relationship exists between San Diego City College's honors program and UCLA through the UCLA Transfer Alliance Program (TAP). This allows for greater connectivity and resource development for helping individual students transfer to the university.[76] Through dedicating more money and personnel to support these partnerships, as well as reevaluating curriculums and centering more effort on problem solving this issue between community college and university professors and administrators, the transfer experience for these California students has been significantly enhanced.[77]

Offering these resources could increase transfer students' confidence. The close relationship Transfer Alliance Program (TAP) directors from community colleges had with university-level staff members allowed for detailed discussions about prospective transfer students and focusing on student progress.[78] Herald Kane said the UCLA Transfer Alliance Program "has provided perhaps the best model to date of a comprehensive intersegmental mechanism for community college-to-university transfer."[79] After one year, the state board "voted to institutionalize the honors program and directed that appropriate resources be supplied," which served as a huge coup.[80]

More recently, in 2011, a unique partnership developed between Michigan's Wayne State University and Macomb Community College, which allowed community college transfer students to graduate from Wayne State with university honors. Macomb Community College students could take courses at both campuses, starting their first year by registering for classes within the Irvin D. Reid Honors College at Wayne State, a research-based institution. Admission was dependent on having a strong academic record, writing an essay, and being evaluated via an interview. One of the perks of the Honors Wayne Direct program was awarding scholarships to these students.[81]

"Macomb transfer students accepted as Wayne State honors transfer students are offered: dedicated advising; special sections of general education courses; designated floors for those wishing to live on campus; and the opportunity to graduate with departmental honors."[82] This program has also won over students and administrators alike in easing the transition process, but some students experience a rude awakening when making the shift from community colleges to universities if partnerships are nonexistent.

TRANSFER SHOCK

Researchers have been increasingly focused on honors transfer students' adjustments to universities, as several key factors account for the success of their integration. Carole Bulakowski and Barbara Townsend conducted a survey of Illinois' College of Lake County honors program students and faculty to elicit their opinions on the program. "Students who completed the honors program also believed that the challenges they met through the honors program prepared them well for the academic rigors that they encountered when they transferred to a four-year college or university."[83]

Similarly, Joseph P. Byrne found that community college honors programs are valuable because they prepare students for the demands of more intense programs at the university level.[84] Attracting more appealing (harder-working) students, some of whom may participate in service projects, encourages some community colleges to find additional merit in offering honors programs.[85]

"Honors programs at community colleges have been shown to prepare the traditionally underserved population of capable students for academic success both at the Associates level and, as transfer students, at the Baccalaureate level."[86] Garrison also noted that students who complete community college honors programs are more likely to graduate, making them more appealing to honors programs at the university level.[87] These community college honors program graduates are typically "guaranteed admission to the accepting institution's honors program or college," but this statement fails to focus on the disparities between the formats of the programs.[88]

What do all of these viewpoints and findings have in common? These perspectives do not fully detail the complexity of the transfer process. While some students, as they indicated, prosper upon transitioning to the university, others flounder. Frankie S. Laanan suggested that many honors transfer students experience difficulty with adapting to more demanding academic standards.[89] Various studies have indicated that upon entering a university, transfer students experience both "transfer shock" and a drop in GPA, though most students recover from this after acclimating.[90]

What types of challenges do honors transfer students face? What happens if a community college honors student transfers to a university, but does not enter an honors college? Does the student then experience fewer challenges and feel more frustrated? Researchers have not yet examined students in these situations. What is clear, however, is that community college honors students who receive faculty support at the two-year community college level but not from faculty members upon arriving at universities may experience a disconnect with their new institutions. Thus students may suffer upon transferring due to lack of personal connections.[91]

Perhaps this may play a role in the startling statistics that demonstrate "only half of the community-college students who indicate a desire to transfer to a four-year institution eventually succeed," according to a U.S. Department of Education report.[92] This could translate to community college honors students as well. Although their intentions to transfer may be strong, lower rates may reflect the difficulties in integrating to a four-year university. Why do they fail?

Stephen J. Handel reasons that perhaps "four-year faculty remain suspicious of the rigor of the community-college curriculum and the apparent lack of an academic culture."[93] Again, this stigma could also be attached to community college honors programs when viewed from the perspectives of honors faculty at four-year universities. This dismissive outlook could prevent critical bonds from forming.

Transfer shock has become a point of study for some researchers interested in analyzing discrepancies. In 1965, John Hills coined the term *transfer shock*, or a GPA drop after community college students enter into traditional four-year universities, and many researchers observed its impact on a majority of these transfer students.[94] Phillips wanted to develop a study to identify if community college honors students experience less transfer shock than their nonhonors peers.[95]

Phillips evaluated students within Texas' Sam Houston State University to eliminate institution variations and to have close access to the participants he polled. The seventy-seven students who participated, all of whom had attended community college, had at least a 3.3 GPA and transferred fifteen or more credit hours from a community college. Half of the students had taken community college honors courses and the other half had not. Phillips was interested in analyzing the GPA difference between university students with a community college honors background and those who lacked it.[96]

Statistical analysis revealed that the mean first-semester GPA of these former honors students was 3.52, while their nonhonors peers had a mean 3.22 GPA.[97] Ironically, both groups of students had the same entering GPA: 3.60, thus placing them at a level playing field.[98] Based on these findings, Phillips concluded that more academically gifted community college students benefit more from honors classes than nonhonors classes.[99] Of course, this is only one example and may not be representative of honors transfer students more generally. More studies at individual institutions—or perhaps a large-scale investigation of transfer students at a state level—should investigate the academic impact of this potential phenomenon.

In this study, community college honors students possessed higher expectations in maintaining time and organization effectively, thus setting them up for additional responsibilities.[100] The results are startling and suggestive of the value of community college honors programs. Yet this cannot be regarded as representative of all honors programs, given the many variables at play. Furthermore, researcher Daniel House found that the level of academic performance—or lack thereof—in which a student transfers to a new institution may influence the degree of transfer shock.[101]

"Previous research has indicated that students who transfer from the community college to the four-year school as juniors earn higher grades, have higher graduation rates, and have lower academic dismissal rates than students who transfer as freshmen or sophomores."[102] This is also telling, in that academic level can figure into students' level of success, though recall that this research did not focus on honors students. The complexities of transfer shock make this a fascinating subject, but only if more studies are conducted in this arena may more of the nuances be revealed.

ADMISSIONS

Among the many variables that determine a student's potential to succeed is being admitted in the first place. Selection into a community college honors program can appear limited and elitist, according to some critics. On the other hand, the restrictions related to admittance can also ensure only the very best can take advantage of honors program benefits. This is a double-edged sword, as students who have the most potential but fall short of meeting the criteria suffer the biggest blow: decreased confidence. Alternatively, those who make the cut but lack the commitment to their education may sabotage their opportunities.

"Critics of community college honors programs believe that, because honors programs use selective admissions criteria, not everyone has access to these programs, which contradicts the community college mission of open access."[103] Ten percent of those community colleges with honors program admitted students based on scores from the SAT, ACT, or both tests. Many community college honors programs required multiple factors to indicate admissibility, Outcalt observed.[104]

For example, high school grades, SAT scores, personal interviews, and evaluations from high school teachers were among the factors taken into account when admitting students into Rockland Community College's honors program.[105] Likewise, a majority of community college honors programs employ selectivity in the students they admit.[106] These multifaceted approaches may prove effective in attaining well-rounded students, but often the students who belong to community college honors programs are far from diverse, as mentioned earlier.

Some honors programs offer courses open to everyone, thus increasing the accessibility.[107] Bell contends that having a mix of students in classrooms can provide "a wonderful recruiting tool for our programs," and assists in spreading honors' ideas to others.[108] This may provide some nonhonors students with the impetus to commit more diligently to their academics and apply to honors programs. For others, this could have incited a more competitive atmosphere in which honors students appeared like "the favorites."

Piney Technical College argued for instituting this format. Its vice president for academic services organized a task force in 2007 aimed at reviewing the honors program.[109] The task force suggested open enrollment as a way to entice potential students to join the honors program.[110] "This would allow more students to join, give faculty a chance to help these students improve academically, and encourage faculty to see the honors college as an open opportunity for all students who were academically motivated."[111]

Catering to academically driven students has been a hallmark of many community college honors programs, essentially the reason why they formed in the first place. New York University professor Richard C. Richardson argued that many academically capable students choose community colleges due to location, family commitments, or other obligations.[112] Honors programs at community colleges have been designed to give the more academically inclined students an outlet to gain more out of their courses, as well as to enhance their image and increase potential connections to universities.[113]

Interestingly, as Mullin stated, "little attention [is] given to the academically advanced students within the community college student body."[114] Only until more recently have community colleges recognized the many subsections that make up their populations—notably the role of academically well-prepared students.[115] More effective honors programs and colleges may wish to consider instituting courses that mix up the student population to include non-honors students to raise the level of honors influence and interest alike.

CONCLUSION

All is not lost for honors transfer students, despite the occasional signals that appear to indicate they remain alone in an ocean of helplessness. These students may possess the basic foundation to transfer to university-level honors programs or colleges, but easily transitioning into the system, and eventually graduating, may be dependent on the guidance and resources provided. If institutions continue to remain disconnected from one another, low admittance rates of transfer students into university-level honors programs or colleges will persist.

Of those who are admitted, disengagement may continue to occur if the program does not accommodate the complex demands on their time and their diverse educational experiences. Some institutions, as evidenced earlier, are leading the way in reducing the disconnect, but more programs must be established nationwide to enhance success among honors transfer students. Honors programs and colleges at all levels in higher education must take these points to heart to ensure a "win-win" scenario.

Their retention of and academic success rates among honors transfer students may grow to become more favorable, which benefits both the students and the institutions. Formulating appropriate modifications to existing honors programs and colleges through composing enhanced partnerships will brighten the potential of students entering "the honors college of tomorrow."

Concurrently, labels must be eliminated. "Two-year colleges are often viewed by legislators as dumping grounds for unprepared students."[116] If these stereotypes persist, the disappointing trends will continue. These community college honors students are no less capable, nor less motivated than their peers who directly enter university-level honors programs or colleges. They are making educational choices to fit their lifestyles, and should the community college honors programs offer valuable tools they can fully utilize, students may be provided a richer groundwork than those who head straight to the university.

Much more research on the topics of community college honors programs, their relationships with university-level honors programs or colleges, and transfer shock in general must be conducted and reviewed by educational experts for more solutions to materialize. The same institutions responsible for building community college honors program students to succeed are also partially liable for students' downfall if these transfers cannot integrate into university-level honors programs or colleges.

This challenge can no longer be a subject left to chance, much like the honors transfer students who are often forgotten by the university-level honors programs or colleges that admit them. Sometimes these shadows fade away, regrettably disappearing into an ocean, an academic honors oblivion, by no choice of their own.

But others reach the surface and find a safety net just beyond the horizon. Honors students must defy the odds in successfully transferring and remove the veils that cover their faces and valuable voices.

Equally so, honors programs and colleges of the future—at both community colleges and universities—must embrace these transfer students' unique backgrounds and experiences through providing adequate articulation agreements and support systems, among other goods, to ensure they do not slip away from public consciousness.

Looking forward, honors education cannot discount the transfer student population, as archaic philosophies that students first starting postsecondary experiences at universities are most important will not survive in this new age of higher education. The future is now, but when these honors programs or colleges begin to reform their approach to transfer students is up to them. Honors transfer students are here to stay, to share their stories, and to perhaps teach their own educators about their growing presence in academia.

KEY IDEAS IN THIS CHAPTER

- Thus far, not enough research has been conducted on honors education within the community college system or those honors students who transition from community colleges to four-year universities.
- Honors programs and colleges articulating agreements for transfer students from community colleges must take systematic and intentional steps to allow flexibility in meeting requirements and recognizing the unique needs of these students.
- Institutions looking for tenable, long-term arrangements that provide equal opportunities for these transfers will build in support structures, guidance, and resources to ensure their success.

NOTES

1. Jeffrey G. Garrison, "Honors, What It Is and What Role It Plays in America's Community Colleges," *Journal of Global Media Studies* 10 (2012): 2.

2. Tod Treat and Thomas C. Barnard, "Seeking Legitimacy: The Community College Mission and the Honors College," *Community College Journal of Research and Practice* 36, no. 9 (2012): 695.

3. Garrison, "Honors, What It Is," 2.

4. Greg Phillips, "The Role of Community College Honors Programs in Reducing Transfer Shock," *Journal of the National Collegiate Honors Council-Online Archive* 146 (2004): 97.

5. Herald R. Kane, "Honors Programs: A Case Study of Transfer Preparation," *New Directions for Community Colleges*, no. 114 (2001): 27.

6. Joseph P. Byrne, "Honors Programs in Community Colleges: A Review of Recent Issues and Literature," *Community College Review* 26, no. 2 (1998): 67.

7. Ibid.

8. Marie T. Huntsinger, "When Isomorphism Fails: Structural Barriers to a Community College Honors Program" (Master's thesis, Arizona State University, 2012), 2.

9. "Community College Honors Programs," *Peterson's*, January 28, 2013, http://www.petersons.com/college-search/community-college-honors-programs.aspx.

10. Treat and Barnard, "Seeking Legitimacy," 696.

11. Charles L. Outcalt, "The Importance of Community College Honors Programs," in *Trends in the Community College Curriculum*, ed. Gwyer Schuyler (San Francisco: Jossey-Bass, 1999), 62–63.

12. Bridget T. Long, "Attracting the Best: The Use of Honors Programs to Compete for Students" (2002), accessed July 15, 2015, http://eric.ed.gov/?id=ED465355, 11.

13. Byrne, "Honors Programs," 67.

14. Frankie Santos Laanan, "Beyond Transfer Shock: Dimensions of Transfer Students' Adjustment," Presentation at the Annual Meeting of the American Educational Research Association Conference, New Orleans, Louisiana, April 24–28, 2000.

15. Byrne, "Honors Programs," 67.

16. Outcalt, "The Importance," 63.

17. Deborah Engelen-Eigels and Janice Levinsohn Milner, "Why Honors Is a Hard Sell in the Community College," *Journal of the National Collegiate Honors Council* (2014): 96.

18. Ibid., 96.

19. Jeffrey Berger, "Honors as a Transformative Experience: The Role of Liberal Arts Honors Programs in Community Colleges," *Journal of College Admission*, no. 194 (2007): 30.

20. Kane, "Honors Programs," 35–36.

21. Ibid., 36.

22. Kane, "Honors Programs," 35.

23. Byrne, "Honors Programs," 67.

24. Berger, "Honors as a Transformative Experience," 31.

25. Phillips, "The Role of Community College," 101.

26. Kane, "Honors Programs," 36.

27. Ibid., 37.

28. Berger, "Honors as a Transformative Experience," 32.

29. Ibid.

30. Ibid.

31. Garrsion, "Honors, What It Is," 4.

32. Ibid., 5.

33. Peter Bahr and Kathy Booth, "What's Completion Got to Do With It?: Using Course-Taking Behavior to Understand Community College Success," *Research and Planning Group for California Community Colleges* (2012): 6, http://www.rpgroup.org/resources/completion-inquiry-guide-and-research-tools.

34. Garrison, "Honors, What It Is," 8.

35. Berger, "Honors as a Transformative Experience," 30.

36. Deborah L. Floyd and Alexandria Holloway, "Prioritizing Service to the Academically Talented: The Honors College," *New Directions for Community Colleges*, no. 136 (2006): 50, http://www.lib.asu.edu.

37. Rosalie Otero and Robert Spurrier, "Assessing and Evaluating Honors Programs and Honors Colleges: A Practical Handbook" (2005): 42, http://www.lib.asu.edu.

38. Kevin J. Dougherty and Barbara Townsend, "Community College Missions: A Theoretical and Historical Perspective," *New Directions for Community Colleges*, no. 136 (2006): 10, http://www.lib.asu.edu.

39. Floyd and Holloway, "Prioritizing Service," 34.

40. Robert D. Bolge, "Identifying and Dealing with Access Barriers at Mercer County Community College" (1994), http://www.lib.asu.edu.

41. Carole Bulakowski and Barbara Townsend, "Evaluation of a Community College Honors Program: Problems and Possibilities," *Community College Journal of Research and Practice* 19, no. 6 (1995): 495, http://www.lib.asu.edu.

42. Garrsion, "Honors, What It Is," 6.

43. Scott R. Furtwengler, "Goal Orientation Does Not Predict Student Participation in a Community College Honors Program" (paper presented at the annual meeting of the Southwest Educational Research Association, San Antonio, Texas, February 7, 2013).

44. Kane, "Honors Programs," 33.

45. Outcalt, "The Importance," 60.

46. Kane, "Honors Programs," 31–32.

47. Ibid., 32.

48. Phillips, "The Role of Community College," 101.

49. Floyd and Holloway, "Prioritizing Service," 46.

50. Garrison, "Honors, What It Is," 9.

51. Outcalt, "The Importance," 60–61.

52. Ibid.

53. Ibid., 61.

54. Ibid., 65.

55. Ibid.

56. Ibid., 66.

57. Ibid., 67.

58. Floyd and Holloway, "Prioritizing Service," 47.

59. Ibid.

60. Ibid., 48–49.

61. Ibid., 49.

62. Ibid., 48.

63. Ibid.

64. Alexandria Holloway, "The Honors College in a Two-Year Setting: Miami Dade College," in *NCHC Monograph Series: The Honors College Phenomenon*, ed. Peter C. Sederberg (Lincoln, NE: National Collegiate Honors Council, 2008), 59.

65. Floyd and Holloway, "Prioritizing Service," 46.

66. Stephen J. Handel, "Second Chance, Not Second Class: A Blueprint for Community-College Transfer," *Change: The Magazine of Higher Learning* 39, no. 5 (2007): 39, http://www.lib.asu.edu.

67. Ibid., 40.

68. Ibid.

69. Ibid., 38.

70. Ibid.

71. Ibid., 40.

72. Ibid., 42.

73. Ibid.

74. Ibid., 44.

75. Ibid.

76. Kane, "Honors Programs," 26.

77. Ibid., 28.

78. Ibid., 30.

79. Ibid., 28.

80. Ibid., 33.

81. "Wayne State and Macomb Community College Sign Historic 'Honors WayneDistrict' and 'Honors Transfer Agreement,'" *Wayne State University Media*, March 24, 2011, accessed July 5, 2014, http://media.wayne.edu/2011/03/24/wayne-state-and-macomb-college-sign-historic.

82. Ibid.

83. Bulakowski and Towsend, "Evaluation of a Community," 491.

84. Byrne, "Honors Programs," 67.

85. Garrison, "Honors, What It Is," 3.

86. Ibid., 7.

87. Ibid., 8.

88. Ibid., 8–9.

89. Frankie S. Laanan, "Transfer Student Adjustment," *New Directions for Community Colleges*, no. 114 (2001): 5, http://www.lib.asu.edu.

90. Ibid., 6–7.

91. Floyd and Holloway, "Prioritizing Service," 50.

92. Handel, "Second Chance, Not Second Class," 38.

93. Ibid., 39.

94. Phillips, "The Role of Community College," 97.

95. Ibid., 97–98.

96. Ibid., 98.

97. Ibid., 99.

98. Ibid., 100.

99. Ibid., 101.

100. Ibid., 102.

101. Edward J. Keeley and Daniel J. House, "Transfer Shock Revisited: A Longitudinal Study" (paper presented at the Association for Institutional Research Annual Forum, Chicago, May 16–19, 1993).

102. Ibid.

103. Treat and Barnard, "Seeking Legitimacy," 697.

104. Outcalt, "The Importance," 63.

105. Robin Wilson, "A Community College Propels Graduates to Top Universities," *The Chronicle of Higher Education* 39, no. 3 (1992), http://www.lib.asu.edu.

106. Floyd and Holloway, "Prioritizing Service," 44

107. Ibid.

108. Gary Bell, "The New Model Education," *Journal of the National Collegiate Honors Council-Online Archive* 62 (2008): 54, http://www.lib.asu.edu.

109. Treat and Barnard, "Seeking Legitimacy," 700–1.

110. Ibid., 704.

111. Ibid.

112. Jeffrey Selingo, "Honors Programs Boom at Community Colleges," *The Chronicle of Higher Education*, May 31, 2002, accessed July 5, 2014, http://chronicle.com/article/Honors-Porgrams-Boom-at/33564.

113. Bulakowski and Townsend, "Evaluation of a Community," 486.

114. Christopher M. Mullin, "Transfer: An Indispensable Part of the Community College Mission," *American Association of Community Colleges Policy Brief 2012-03PBL* (2012): 5, http://www.lib.asu.edu.

115. Phillips, "The Role of Community College," 97.

116. Selingo, "Honors Programs Boom."

Chapter Four

Honors Program Innovation and the Role of Technology

A Case Study of Honors e-Portfolios

Maureen Kelleher and Lauren Pouchak

THE E-PORTFOLIO AND BEYOND THE CLASSROOM LEARNING

Learning portfolios have been used in educational settings since the 1960s. Starting in the 1980s, they began to be used more extensively in writing-intensive majors such as English and communication studies and art-related fields. In these early models, students collected their work, made decisions about which work should be featured, and incorporated a reflective component to the process as part of the portfolio. By the mid-1990s, portfolio models became especially popular in schools of education in which students could reflect their competencies as they prepared for careers as teachers.[1]

As currently envisioned, learning portfolios are seen as a means for assessing "education through learning artifacts and outcomes . . . instead of grades and graduation rates" and a way of providing evidence of faculty facilitating "students in authoring their own learning."[2] There are several distinct assets to student-driven portfolio models, including the emphasis on learning, the provision of a structure for the experience, and the shift to student agency.[3]

The use of e-Portfolios (EPs) contributes to future possibilities in honors education because in a fundamental way they challenge the limits of the traditional classroom learning model and enable a more inclusive, holistic view of the higher education experience. EPs build on the parameters of the traditional learning portfolio with their emphasis on reflection and exchange to capture the serendipitous and the "long-haul" of an undergraduate's *learning life*. Through the use of an online submission process, EPs broaden the ability of others, including peers, to read student work. EPs expand the boundaries and capacities of intellectual growth and exchange beyond the classroom because they are neither limited by time (that is, classroom schedule) nor traditional work space (that is, the classroom, the library, the dorm room).

Certainly, as they are envisioned, the use of learning portfolios helps capture the goals of an honors education through unique opportunities for reflection and integration. Honors programs emphasize interdisciplinarity, the support of global experiences, the recognition of the importance of experiential learning, and the commitment to civic engagement. Through curriculum innovation, honors programs try to facilitate links throughout the undergraduate experience. Innovative use of learning portfolios supports the opportunity for those links to be actualized.

John Zubizarreta, who often writes on honors education, pushes the potential even further by arguing that learning portfolios could move beyond the idea of mere "collection and organizing devices"[4] toward a process that could have implications for "student's overall cognitive, social, ethical, and spiritual development."[5] Thus for Zubizarreta and others there is an important role played by the "collaborative mentor who helps provide feedback in making decisions about purpose, content, format and selectivity."[6] As a result, critical components include not only documentation of materials, but also student reflection and a collaborative engagement. These components would resonate with an EP model.

Although traditional pen-and-paper learning portfolios have been used successfully on college campuses for some time, the transition to EPs occurred approximately in 2003.[7] Like traditional learning portfolios before them, EPs were intended "to provide long-term storage for student work beyond the scope of their college career . . . and assessment opportunities."[8] EPs could replicate the emphasis of learning portfolios on "collection, selection, and reflection." When the electronic element was introduced into the learning portfolio model, the possibilities for linkages and interactivity and the opportunity for social action increased exponentially.[9]

The EP is an online system that students can use to store materials connected to their undergraduate experience. At a minimum, the EP provides a virtual space where students can *stash* materials collected during their undergraduate years. At their best, EPs offer the potential to provide "an evidence-based, professional account of . . . emerging knowledge, skills, and dispositions"[10] of self-awareness and reflection. Through the use of digital technologies, EPs offer students the opportunity to "make unique linkages, connections, and reflections among multiple experiences and artifacts."[11]

Christopher R. Corley and John Zubizarreta note that EPs offer students a "robust and flexible mechanism."[12] By "collecting multiple types of selective evidence of learning," students can actively engage "in a critically reflective process."[13] EPs, for example, allow students the capacity to integrate multimedia materials in ways not effectively allowed by traditional portfolios.

In addition, materials can be catalogued in ways that allow student knowledge acquisition to be tracked. As students construct their own portfolios, they begin to make connections between "experiences, skills and artifacts and of making these connections visible to readers" and themselves.[14] Thus they engage in what Helen L. Chen and Tracy Penny Light term "folio thinking."[15] Students are given the opportunity to assume responsibility for their own "success, intellectual growth, and individual development."[16]

That opportunity to self-construct a portfolio with its emphasis on internal linkages and connections contributes to the student's sense of ownership not just of their work, but also of a summative assessment of their learning. They are, in essence, active creators rather than passive revivers of that assessment.[17]

In addition, EPs provide opportunities to share materials with many other audience groups: not just faculty, but also peers, prospective employers, and parents.[18] The linking and sharing capacities of EPs create the potential for an enhanced *dialogue* between students and their professors and advisors. That dialogue can be both retrospective—looking back on activities and courses completed—as well as anticipatory—looking forward with "intent to plan in documents such as the resume."[19]

The dialogue at the core of EPs promotes "transparency, accountability, and communication" between a broad constituency: "students, faculty, staff, administrators, and accrediting and professional bodies."[20] This transparency/accountability is built by "mapping individual student work . . . progressively from individual courses to goals at the department or program, college, institutional, system and national levels."[21] This dialogue helps transform EPs from collections of completed work to active reflections situated in the present regarding the students' plans for future educational tasks and aspirations.

Clearly, EPs serve individual classroom needs where the focus can be on teaching (the faculty member), learning (the student), and the curriculum. All of these components can also have implications for assessment and advising and even major curriculum reforms.[22] This emphasis is framed by the understanding that not all students have strong technology skills and as a result, in implementing such an initiative, an understanding of what skills students need in order to effectively use this model relies on class support targeted to specific learning needs, or what Chen and Light term "individual scaffolding."[23]

EPs offer the opportunity to "capture, represent, and demonstrate learning outcomes, thus contributing to a more efficient and more meaningful overall assessment system—one that highlights the value of personal reflection and self-assessment for individual students."[24] The "various assessment needs of faculty, departments, programs and institutions" can be enhanced by their effective implementation.[25]

HONORS AND EPS: A CASE STUDY OF THREE PROGRAMS

The educational philosophy of EPs undergirds the implementation process that programs undergo in developing this initiative. The focus, for the purpose of this chapter, is on EP implementation in honors programs. Honors programs provide a unique role in the development and distribution of an EP initiative on campus.

First, honors programs are in a unique position to test drive such an initiative. Second, honors programs often have a shared/required first-year course that all students take, thus enhancing the possibility of a uniform EP training experience. Third, honors programs are by their nature more "intrusive" units, often not only engaging with the academic life of the student, but also offering comprehensive services that include specialized/mandatory advising.

This frequent student/staff interaction combined with the potential for requiring EPs as part of an honors graduation requirement for distinction positions honors programs as excellent EP sites on individual campuses. Honors programs can also lead the way to innovation transfer across the larger campus community.

The challenges and opportunities of redesigning honors programs for the "digital age" have attracted particular attention
through a special edition of the *Journal of the National Collegiate
Honors Council*.[26] The implementation of EPs into honors programs has also been addressed in numerous recent articles that
primarily focus on either one course or one campus.[27]

This chapter adds to the literature by focusing on a case study of
three large universities that successfully implemented EPs in their
honors programs. This case study illustrates not only the cross-
disciplinary effectiveness of such an initiative, but also the feasibility of implementing an EP initiative in large honors programs and
the longitudinal contribution of EPs over the course of the undergraduate experience. This chapter also addresses the incidental
finding that other significant issues come to the fore that are beyond the original goals of EP implementation that focus primarily
on teaching, learning, and assessment issues.

The following case study of honors programs using EPs will
focus on their integration of EPs into their programs. Through the
case, one can see both how the projects were locally envisioned and
implemented and the way they have incorporated certain components of the EP model into the core goals of their particular program.

Providing a technical system to support students making connections between their experiences inside and outside of their major and inside and outside of the classroom helps to situate students
to develop a curiosity about and understanding of the connected-
ness between their wide range of undergraduate experiences, including honors. EPs serve as a vehicle for making clear the challenges students face and the progress they make during those years.
EPs also help students to develop an understanding of the links and
building blocks that become part of an effective experience because
at their core they require a commitment to reflection.

The University of Cincinnati (UC), the University of Washington–Seattle (UW), and Northeastern University (NU) were selected for study. Each program has been using EPs for at least four years (for a comparative profile of the three schools, see table 4.1). The case study was developed through a series of interviews with senior staff at each of the three campuses. Campuses were chosen based on program size, presentations at national honors meetings regarding EP initiatives, and professional conversations as the initiative was developed on home campuses.

The authors conducted semi-structured interviews. Open-ended questions regarding the adoption and implementation of EPs offered the opportunity to create a dialogue between researchers and subjects that can surface deep insights and allow for the possibility of unanticipated results.[28] In all cases, senior staff were given drafts of the cases to review for corrections and additional materials if appropriate. All direct quotes from honors program staff come from these interviews.

In addition, the honors program websites of all three campuses were reviewed. One campus is located on the West Coast, one in the Midwest, and the last on the East Coast. What they all share is the commitment to innovation in undergraduate education—part of the underlying mantra of honors work. The introduction and use of EPs is an example of this innovation.

INTRODUCING THE EP INITIATIVE

EPs offer students a platform for integrating their experiences. UC staff noted that students were having "high impact experiences" but were not integrating them in any meaningful way. The EP requirement was seen as a way for them to both reflect on their learning and try to create some sort of cohesive story. On the program's website, the EP experience is framed by offering students a range of opportunities. At UC, students may reflect on their collegiate

Table 4.1.   Case studies at a glance

	University of Cincinnati	University of Washington–Seattle	Northeastern University
Nature of institution	Public	Public	Private
Total full-time undergraduate enrollment	25,000	29,754	13,000
Honors program founding	1991	Late 1980s	1987
Scope of honors	University-wide	Mixed: departmental and college/ interdisciplinary	University-wide
Honors program enrollment	1,300	1,374	2,900
Launch of EP	2008	2010	2011
Honors introductory course with EP training	Yes	Yes	Yes
Use of honors learning portfolio prior to EP	No	No	No
Cooperative education: Work experience integrated into undergraduate course work	Yes	No	Yes

experiences, establish links between their curricular and co-curricular involvement, integrate learning, and evaluate their academic, personal, and professional identities. [29]

The impetus for the EP initiative at NU is also to help students tie the disparate parts of an undergraduate experience into a more cohesive whole that students could see developing during their time on campus. Like the other programs, NU's EPs are also seen as a way of supplementing traditional academic advising by offering advisors an opportunity to evaluate students' overall development at appropriate junctures in their undergraduate careers. "The e-Portfolio is also an *advising tool*," the NU webpage notes, "a way for honors staff to effectively understand your academic and experiential trajectory."[30]

All of the programs emphasize the benefits of an EP in allowing students to present themselves holistically to others. "The Honors Portfolio is a web-based collection of artifacts and reflective writing that documents and contextualizes your undergraduate experience," notes the UW honors program webpage, "allowing you to tell your UW Honors story to your peers, friends, family, current and future mentors and employers, and graduate school admissions board."[31] Adds UC, the EPs offer the opportunity for "communicating the integration of learning to various university audiences."[32]

Still, the main beneficiary of the program is presented as the individual student. "The most important audience, however, is yourself," notes UW.[33] At UC, honors advising staff are assigned a caseload of student EPs to review and provide student feedback during the summer months. Often advisors push students to ask themselves more reflective questions. The range of the artifacts submitted by students through their EPs is wide. UC advisors find that some students are "fully immersed, and use it to talk about relationships with family and friends and student organizations and activities they are involved with as well as their honors experiences."

For advisors at UW, gaining insight into students' "Ah Ha!" moments help them understand how profound some of the undergraduate experiences are. For example, students "didn't know that 'failure' informs experience later on," and now begin to connect their "process of education to not see classes as finite."

UW staff commented that sometimes students' reflections indicate a lack of interest or motivation toward their EP assignments, "not understanding how the portfolio fits into their practical CV needs." EPs position advisors to make a timely intervention that may provide students "opportunities to work through the benefits of reflecting more broadly and . . . for a variety of purposes [including future] graduate programs, careers, scholarships, [and] telling their story to family and friends."

EPs have also provided honors personnel insight into what might be thought of as "missed opportunities." As a result, UC staff developed second-year group sessions to help students think of ways to get involved. "Looking at student development theory and how students are making sense of interpersonal and personal cognitive development, we recognized that the second year is an important time when students are making sense of identities."

The UC honors program is not only concerned with helping students "harness their own talents," but also with recognizing the power of the larger honors community and the impact that it can make. Staff there acknowledge the importance for honors programs to help support students who are "conscious and considerate and understand the importance of thinking across disciplines." But also staff are cognizant of issues of privilege and power and "who is taking tests to succeed and ending up in honors programs." Such acknowledgment transcends all three programs. EPs may play an important role in understanding how students look at these issues.

The honors program at NU agrees. "The Honors Portfolio is an opportunity to continue exploring your own capacities within the world." By allowing students a means of integrating "your years on campus," reflecting on "the different opportunities of classroom and experiential learning afforded by your time here," and representing "yourself and your work in a meaningful way," the NU program adds, EPs become "the basis for tracing your educational *arc*—tying together your earliest work in honors, your work in your major, advanced research for Honors in the Discipline and your upper-class capstone."[34]

LESSONS LEARNED

Honors staff are often surprised by the breadth and depth of reflections manifest in the students' EPs. Some of the submissions at UC, for instance, touch on outside-the-classroom activities such as "roommate struggles, major changes, how this has impacted on a student's sense of identity." Given both what and how much students will disclose, the EPs offer "the best picture of what college life looks like to students."

UC staff sometimes notice dissonance between formal course evaluations and student EP reflections. Specifically, EPs raise more insightful comments on individual course experiences that are less likely to be found on a university-sponsored course evaluation system. A sense of what is happening in particular classrooms is always something that is raised in individual advising meetings, and these conversations provide supplemental information on student learning.

Beyond formal evaluations and conversations, EPs provide advisors with a third source of information. The advisors' assessment of the e-portfolios each year has enriched the UC honors program's insight into student perspectives on faculty effectiveness and what students are reporting in terms of personal needs in addition to academic growth.

Students at UW also write about their struggles, and as a result advisors are positioned to offer both support and direction. In some cases, students underrepresented in honors and across UW express a "disconnect" to the larger honors/university community. Students may articulate how difficult it is to find where they fit in. Honors staff are then positioned to help these students find an expanded support community on campus.

The transformative changes students experience are illustrated to the NU staff by a discussion of their experiences in the upperclass seminar. There they talk about how they learn to "articulate transitions they are going through" in their EP reflections. They have also learned about themselves as people, sometimes articulating the "profound" impact of their experiences in their EP reflections.

At NU the early requirement of a first-year reflection entry has shifted more explicitly to integrate the developmental advising undertaken by honors advisors. "Now students do one reflection on their academic vision and in reading them, we learn about what they have brought to the university." Students develop an initial vision at the beginning of their first semester and then revise it at the end of their first semester.

The "academic vision assignment is a way for staff to look at curriculum development and social needs." Personal issues are brought up in student reflections, and as a result advisors can reach out to students articulating either general dissatisfaction/unhappiness or depression. NU staff believe that through the EPs "we are able to learn about these issues and can help." There are also students who do not take things seriously or "don't buy into the larger conversations. We . . . see what we can do to help situate them better."

Disclosure raises concerns about privacy, which is addressed at UC. Staff work with students who wish to disclose information, but also want to protect their public presence by not presenting some information to a wider audience. Such sensitivity to student needs goes almost hand in hand with asking students to write about themselves.

CHALLENGES

Honors programs are designed to be cross-college initiatives. At the same time, university colleges tend to operate in quite separate spheres from one another. As a result, students often do not interact much with students outside of their own college. UC honors staff try to create a more integrated community in their classroom opportunities and also employ other strategies such as mixing up third-year group advising experiences with students from different colleges.

One tension that became clear to UW honors program advisors was in the EP messaging. On the one hand there are clearly articulated categories, a formal structure, and a series of requirements. On the other hand, students are also encouraged to "take ownership of their portfolios." As a result, there is a "tension between making the portfolio a reflection of their experiences . . . and the boundaries of structural expectations." Privacy functions built in as EP options allow students to have personal ownership and also to meet larger honors program requirements.

With the largest honors program enrollment in our sample (2,900 students), the NU honors program faced a logistical challenge of trying to effectively facilitate training of the entering class on how to set up and use EP resources. The assumption was that if students could not be effectively trained, the larger goals of teaching, learning, and assessment were not possible to actualize. In 2013, the logistics of the training began to work out smoothly (a three-year process including the pilot year).

Sometimes the "buy-in" piece to the EPs initiative is a struggle. Anecdotal evidence indicates that some students see the learning portfolio as fluff or an unnecessary requirement, just writing "another essay." There also can be a lack of depth. Other students, ironically, actually write too much, and honors staff at UC help them learn how to be more concise; they write "so much that it is not accessible to an external audience."

Because of the nature of some of the cooperative education work experiences at both NU and UC (that is, in settings with clients or research settings), sometimes students cannot discuss their work experiences or perhaps inappropriately use materials from their workplace without attribution. Advising staff can help students work through these issues in an effective manner.

NEXT STEPS

At UC, the main focus is on the senior honors exit course. Staff want to focus on "how to manage and streamline it" without compromising the quality of the experience. The honors staff are responding to this concern by gathering people together for a larger network: getting honors faculty to require course reflections, and more ambitiously expanding the EP requirements into nonhonors courses. They also have a unique resource for their advanced class—a one-credit course on public speaking that helps prepare students for the advanced honors presentations.

UC also envisions a number of additional next steps for their initiative. There is a real potential to create a more unified campus-wide portfolio initiative in which the honors requirements would essentially be a "portfolio within a portfolio: and a cross campus synergy could be fueled by looking at other campus sites." This would be an ambitious undertaking, but might well be actualized in the future.

Honors staff at NU are interested in understanding what students are learning about themselves as people. A clearer sense of the developmental voice might be more evident by the time they are seniors. Beyond curriculum and advising implications, honors staff see program initiatives also emerging from knowledge gained through the EPs. At NU, one example is a graduate school–focused "speed dating" program that gives undergraduates a chance to meet with locally based graduate students. In addition, EPs have expanded connections made to offices like the crisis intervention office on campus and residential life.

When they think of the larger conversations in the national honors community, staff at both UC and UW are interested in the "rebranding of honors." UW staff, for instance, are concerned about not reaching the boundaries of the university community because of the "elite model" of honors education. "This is a different world; we are not Sputnik driven like 1963!" What they are looking at is the "position, entitlement and the deconstruction of honors." That is an ambitious and also a timely mantra for honors educators.

NU staff are considering ways support should be made available to seniors as they complete their EP assignment in order to be awarded honors distinction. Specifically, what should the exit process look like? Ideas under consideration include whether there will a course, a series of workshops, alignment with other units on campus such as career services, and/or other possible exit strategies.

In addition, at NU, a clearer link needs to be made with honors faculty in terms of facilitating awareness of the EP initiative, targeting training in this strategy for interested faculty, and getting a more robust buy-in to this initiative that clearly links honors curriculum with honors advising and student development goals. Longer-term goals include the viability of extending this initiative beyond honors.

CHALLENGES AND COSTS OF THE EP MODEL

When deciding to start an EP initiative, it is wise to be aware of some of the particular challenges of this electronic model.[35] A real concern is where EP information is located. For example, many EP initiatives occur at the individual course level and as a result focus on course reflection (a teaching and learning emphasis). Other materials are gathered as part of a package to present to potential employers and therefore reflect skills that make a student a likely candidate for employment.

Another concern revolves around who has access to the information. Many schools contract with server systems or use EP software that is freely available online. Some faculty allow students to choose systems that most reflect the types of materials or artifacts they want to store and there may be considerable variance depending on major. Once a system is chosen, questions arise as to long-term access. Do students have access after they graduate or if they drop out of school? Can faculty and/or staff regularly access the materials? What happens in terms of student privacy if the materials are solicited for assessment purposes? These are realistic concerns.[36]

There are EP models that exist for campuses with few resources. These initiatives are more likely to emerge at the individual course level led by faculty who are interested in assessing the effectiveness of the classroom experience they are providing their students. There are also EP initiatives that have been adopted at the departmental, programmatic, or campus level. These initiatives require a more robust resource allocation and commitment among a number of actors beyond individual students and faculty.[37]

Many students arrive on campus with core technical skills. However, training in aspects of EPs must be offered in order for students to successfully develop and maintain their EP site. Given the technical expertise that some students bring to campus, a real concern occurs when faculty and/or support staff lag behind. Students can also experience technical problems. This can come about because of overconfidence or the wide range of uploaded materials that go beyond reflective essays. Clearly, an ambitious initiative with a wide range of actors involved requires sophisticated resource sharing.[38]

Keith Wetzel and Neal Strudler discovered that, even at schools with EP initiatives that had been in place for several years, students had concerns that clustered around "program implementation, access to and reliability of technology, and issues of time and effort expended."[39] For these students, there was general consensus on the value of the reflection component of the effort and agreement that there was an improvement of technology skills and potential for employment opportunities. However, students found the potential for "reflection overkill," that is, the number and complexity of required reflections could be unreasonable from their perspective.[40]

Students raise other concerns with EPs ranging from clarity of purpose of the assignments such as employing helpful feedback, and the ease of using the portfolio system, to whether faculty were actually providing the feedback or whether faculty were just checking submissions "based on completeness rather than the quality of the content."[41] To address these concerns, it is important to acknowledge the role of students as stakeholders. This student status becomes a critical component in the implementation and improvement of both policy and practice.

Concern also exists regarding the actual impact of EPs on learning and achievement. According to Philip Abrami and Helen Barrett, evidence to date supporting these accomplishments is lean. In part this is because there is a lack of systematic data. They concede that there is a sense that there will be certain situations in which EPs are more effective than in other situations depending on program goals or population served.[42]

What are the factors that may influence outcomes? In addition to the previously mentioned factors of ability level and expertise, Abrami and Barrett raise issues such as gender as creating barriers.[43] Additional issues can also be added, such as class background and ease of access to computing equipment. These and many other factors impact whether EPs are effective.

Finally, there is concern with the role that online assessment might play in changing the nature of the fundamental goals of a learning portfolio experience.

For example, Barrett illustrates the differences between EPs and assessment management. First, the purpose of EPs is to focus on learning, assessment, and potential employment. The purpose of assessment management is to focus on formative and summative assessment. Second, the locus of control of EPs is student-centered, while assessment management is institution-centered.[44] She goes on to reflect that "if assessment components are incorporated into the e-Portfolio system, a balancing act is required that meets needs accountability, combined with the importance of the reflective portfolio component."[45]

Certainly there are strong "theoretical arguments for the use of ePortfolios . . . [including] improved learning outcomes, and increased knowledge."[46] Lauren H. Bryant and Jessica R. Chittum point to the "plausibility" that EPs can contribute to student learning. However, they argue that sometimes it is difficult to determine whether learning occurs because of the role played by EPs or because of a particular course structure. They also found that "there are substantial gaps in the literature, and the adoption of ePortfolio continues to outpace our knowledge of its effectiveness and appropriate use."[47]

BEYOND TEACHING, LEARNING, AND ASSESSMENT: STUDENTS IN A CHANGING WORLD

Although it is appropriate to critique emerging EP initiatives, there is also considerable untapped potential. One of the less obvious implications of EP adoptions is to go much further than the fundamental goals of EPs that reside in the teaching/learning/assessment trifecta. This trio, of course, provides the foundation of both learning portfolios and EPs. With the introduction of online access, researchers are becoming aware of other possibilities, some of which were mentioned in the case study. Future research could extend beyond those teaching/learning/assessment goals and impact honors programs in significant ways.

There is already research pushing the parameters of established EP goals. Emerging research is focusing on more complex goals exploring such issues such as identity,[48] audience,[49] community/culture,[50] and race.[51] There remains the possibility of using the implementation of EPs as a vehicle to study student lives in a more systematic, developmentally appropriate, and inclusive manner. This possibility may help honors programs assess the transformational change that is happening in higher education and help contribute to mapping future innovative directions.

Significant historical research exists in higher education that has shed light on student life and both directly and indirectly shaped student services, education policy,[52] and a better understanding of this life stage.[53] More recent research has focused on issues of gender and love,[54] race and college admissions,[55] mental health,[56] campus violence,[57] class,[58] and the loss of a meaningful educational experience.[59]

The use of EPs can enrich that understanding of campus life and experiences. Through the analysis of EPs, honors educators gain insights provided by students into issues such as social isolation (sometimes related to issues of race and class) and depression. Because EPs integrate technologies that are already part of student life (that is, Facebook and Twitter), educators are establishing a unique contact with students that could begin to cast a larger light on contemporary college students' *lived lives*.

Established development models used to study children could help inform analysis of EPs and the insights provided by student voices. Glen H. Elder and colleagues' 1993 cross-disciplinary model of development within a larger framework of historical time seems especially promising.[60] Through the lens of the honors community and the *coming of age stories* as reflected in students' EPs, honors programs are positioned to contribute to the discussion of timely and provocative issues in higher education, such as class/race/diversity, campus violence, and debates such as those revolving around Title IX concerns and campus sexual assaults.

CONCLUSION: LEVERAGING EPS IN AN HONORS SETTING

Although the use of EPs has the potential to change the way honors educators understand contemporary higher education issues, the immediate goal is to impact learning. In particular, EPs provide a portal for students to explore issues of identity: "expressing oneself in relationship to the other."[61] By providing space for student reflection, the opportunity emerges to "create an online representation of their narrative . . . in relation to, and through conversation, with others."[62]

Current K–12 systems, with their emphasis on "twenty-first century skills," commit to a better understanding of cyclical learning that includes failure as a component of that process.[63] Honors programs encourage students to explore and take risks. EPs can become one such place where that exploration is tempered by insight and hindsight. Students become adept at "folio thinking"[64] by establishing "a habit of building connections among experiences, skills and artifacts."[65]

As a cross-college unit representing students from all majors, an honors program is able to harness a comprehensive understanding of the usefulness of an EP initiative. Through assessment, an individual honors unit could help shift program innovation by developing transferable rubrics.

The potential of EPs in the honors curriculum, their contribution to the development of both a sense of the academic and personal *self*, and the potential for expansion to the larger campus makes the adoption of EPs in honors programs one worth serious consideration. The technology is readily available.

The idea of supporting students during their undergraduate years through both their successes and failures is critical. The understanding of the importance of examples of student work and the commitment to a challenging and comprehensive honors experience (linking academic, social, cultural, and residential experiences situated in a particular time and space) allows educators to not only better understand and work with students, but also to better understand and contribute to campus and beyond.

This chapter has provided an overview of some of the core issues and possible directions that either a shift to or development of an EP initiative could take. There is widespread adoption of the learning portfolio model and the uses of reflection in honors education. EPs offer a clear next step in the expanding possibilities in honors of intellectual exchange that is not limited by a single course in a particular semester. This potential exchange becomes more open-ended, fluid, and responsive for students, their peers, and faculty and provides a new way to grow, integrate, and challenge. Honors educators are fueled in this process by the curiosity and ambition of our honors students.

KEY IDEAS IN THIS CHAPTER

- e-Portfolios (EPs) offer a next step in expanding the possibilities of honors education.
- EPs provide opportunity for an intellectual exchange not limited by a single course in a particular semester but reflective of an arc of learning and the attainment of specific skills, talents, and dispositions.
- EPs broaden the way that honors graduates can showcase their educational and intellectual development, enabling students to integrate a broader array of experiences, many occurring beyond the classroom.

NOTES

1. George Lorenzo and John Ittelson, "An Overview of e-Portfolios," *Educause Learning Initiative* 1 (2005): 1–27.

2. Celeste Flowles Nguyen, "The ePortfolio as a Living Portal: A Medium for Student Learning, Identity, and Assessment," *International Journal of ePortfolio* 3, no. 2 (2013): 135.

3. Lee Shulman, "With Portfolio in Hand: Validating the New Teacher Professionalism," in *Teacher Portfolios: A Theoretical Activity*, ed. Nona Lyons (New York: Teachers College Press, 1998), 23–37.

4. John Zubizarreta, *The Learning Portfolio: Reflective Practice for Improving Student Learning*, second edition (San Francisco, CA: John Wiley and Sons, 2009), 5.

5. Ibid.

6. Ibid., 21.

7. Helen L. Chen and Tracy Penny Light, *Electronic Portfolios and Student Success: Effectiveness, Efficiency, and Learning* (Washington, DC: Association of American Colleges and Universities, 2010), 1–38.

8. Kelly Parkes et al., "ePortfolio as a Measure of Reflective Practice," *International Journal of ePortfolio* 3, no. 2 (2013): 99.

9. Kathleen Blake Yancey, "Digitized Student Portfolios," in *Electronic Portfolios: Emerging Practices in Student, Faculty, and Institutional Learning*, ed. Barbara L. Cambridge et al. □(Washington, DC: American Association for Higher Education, 2001), 20.

10. Parkes et al., "ePortfolio as a Measure of Reflective Practice," 99.

11. Ibid., 101.

12. Christopher R. Corley and John Zubizarreta, "The Power and Utility of Reflective Learning Portfolios in Honors," *Journal of the National Collegiate Honors Council*, no. 1 (2012): 63.

13. Ibid.

14. Maria Antonietta Impedovo et al., "Developing Codebooks as a New Tool to Analyze Students' ePortfolios," *International Journal of ePortfolio* 3, no. 2 (2013): 162.

15. Chen and Light, *Electronic Portfolios and Student Success*, 1.

16. Ibid.

17. See Impedovo et al., "Developing Codebooks as a New Tool to Analyze Students' ePortfolios"; Lee Shulman, "With Portfolio in Hand"; Chen and Light, *Electronic Portfolios and Student Success*, 1–38.

18. See Philip Abrami and Helen Barrett, "Directions for Research and Development on Electronic Portfolios," *Canadian Journal of Learning and Technology/La revue canadienne de l'apprentissage et de la technologie* 31, no. 3 (2005): n.p.; Chris Gallagher and Laurie L. Poklop, "ePortfolios and Audience: Teaching a Critical Twenty-First Century Skill," *International Journal ePortfolio* 4, no. 1 (2014): 7–20.

19. Yancey, "Digitized Student Portfolios," 23.

20. Chen and Light, *Electronic Portfolios and Student Success*, 5.

21. Ibid.

22. Yancey, "Digitized Student Portfolios."

23. Chen and Light, *Electronic Portfolios and Student Success*, 9.

24. Ibid., 27.

25. Ibid.

26. "Honors in the Digital Age: Special Issue," *Journal of the National Collegiate Honors Council* 10, no. 2 (Fall/Winter 2009).

27. See Victoria Bocchicchio, "The Senior Honors Portfolio," in *The Learning Portfolio: Reflective Practice for Improving Student Learning*, ed. John Zubizarreta (Boston: Anker Publishing Co., Inc., 2004), 64–68; Earl Brown Jr., "Demonstrating Mastery Through an Honors Portfolio," in *The Learning Portfolio*, 76–82; Candee C. Chambers, "Portfolios Within an Honors Program: The Honors Preparation Year and Beyond," in *The Learning Portfolio*, 87–91.

28. Jack K. Fordyce and Raymond Weil, "Methods for Finding Out What's Going On," in *Organization Development: Theory, Practice, and Research*, ed. Wendell L. French et al. (Dallas, TX: Business Publications, 2006), 121–29.

29. "University Honors Program Learning Portfolios," *University of Cincinnati*, accessed June 29, 2015, https://www.uc.edu/honors/eportfolios.html.

30. "Honors e-Portfolio," *Northeastern University Honors Program*, accessed June 29, 2015, http://www.northeastern.edu/honors/academics-3/honors-e-porfolio.

31. "The Honors Portfolio," *University Honors Department*, accessed June 29, 2015, http://depts.washington.edu/uwhonors/reqs/portfolio.

32. "University Honors Program Learning Portfolios," *University of Cincinnati*.

33. "The Honors Portfolio," *University Honors Department*.

34. "Honors e-Portfolio," *Northeastern University Honors Program*.

35. Lorenzo and Ittelson, "An Overview of e-Portfolios"; Yancey, "Digitized Student Portfolios."

36. Yancey, "Digitized Student Portfolios."

37. Keith Wetzel and Neal Strudler, "Costs and Benefits of Electronic Portfolios in Teacher Education: Student Voices," *Journal of Computing in Teacher Education* 22, no. 3 (2006), 99–108.

38. Yancey, "Digitized Student Portfolios."

39. Wetzel and Strudler, "Costs and Benefits of Electronic Portfolios in Teacher Education," 101.

40. Ibid., 106.

41. Ibid., 107.

42. Abrami and Barrett, "Directions for Research and Development on Electronic Portfolios."

43. Ibid.

44. Helen Barrett, "Differentiating Electronic Portfolios and Online Assessment Management Systems," *Society for Information Technology and Teacher Education International Conference*, no. 1 (2004): 46–50.

45. Ibid.

46. Lauren H. Bryant and Jessica R. Chittum, "ePortfolio Effectiveness: A(n Ill-Fated) Search for Empirical Support," *International Journal of ePortfolio* 3, no. 2 (2013): 189.

47. Ibid., 195.

48. Nguyen, "The ePortfolio as a Living Portal."

49. Gallagher and Poklop, "ePortfolios and Audience."

50. Elaine J. Yuan, "A Culturalist Critique of 'Online Community' in New Media Studies," *New Media and Society* 15, no. 5 (2013): 665–79.

51. Karen Singer-Freeman et al., "ePortfolios Reveal an Emerging Community of Underrepresented Minority Scholars," *International Journal of ePortfolio* 4, no. 1 (2014): 85–94.

52. Howard S. Becker et al., *Boys in White: Student Culture in Medical School* (Chicago: University of Chicago Press, 1961).

53. Howard S. Becker et al., *Making the Grade: The Academic Side of College Life* (Piscataway, NJ: Transaction Publishers, 1968).

54. Dorothy C. Holland, *Educated in Romance: Women, Achievement, and College Culture* (Chicago: University of Chicago Press, 1990).

55. William G. Bowen and Derek Bok, *The Shape of the River: Long-Term Consequences of Considering Race in College and University Admissions* (Princeton, NJ: Princeton University Press, 1998).

56. Richard Kadison and Theresa Foy DiGeronimo, *College of the Overwhelmed: The Campus Mental Health Crisis and What to Do About It* (San Francisco, CA: Jossey Bass, 2004).

57. Mass Shootings at Virginia Tech (April 16, 2007). Report of the Review Panel presented to Governor Kaine, Commonwealth of Virginia, August 2007.

58. Elizabeth A. Armstrong and Laura T. Hamilton, *Paying for the Party* (Cambridge, MA: Harvard University Press, 2013).

59. William Deresiewicz, *Excellent Sheep: The Miseducation of the American Elite and the Way to a Meaningful Life* (New York: Simon and Schuster, 2014).

60. Glen H. Elder et al., eds., *Children in Time and Place: Developmental and Historical Insights* (Cambridge: Cambridge University Press, 1994).

61. Nguyen, "The ePortfolio as a Living Portal," 135.

62. Ibid., 146.

63. Bryant and Chittum, "ePortfolio Effectiveness: A(n Ill-Fated) Search for Empirical Support."

64. Chen and Light, *Electronic Portfolios and Student Success*, 1.

65. Impedovo et al., "Developing Codebooks as a New Tool to Analyze Students' ePortfolios," 162.

Chapter Five

Honors in a Cross-National Context

Scotland's Master of Arts with Honors

Darren J. Reid

How can honors practitioners and administrators learn from taking the time to explore approaches to honors found in countries across the world? The phrase *honors education* is one heard on college and university campuses throughout the United States, yet there is enormous diversity in what constitutes an effective honors program or college. In its most generic form, honors is used to describe a pedagogical approach to higher education that combines in-class and extracurricular activities that are measurably broader, deeper, and more complex than the learning experiences typically found at the undergraduate level.[1]

Honors programs and colleges seek to provide *gifted* or *superior* undergraduate students with a "more individualized educational experience . . . that focuses on the creation of knowledge more than its mere reproduction."[2] In order to achieve this objective, honors students are educated using techniques associated with the *Socratic method*; for example, small, discussion-based tutorials, independent study, and the promotion of a close student-teacher relationship before, within, and outside of the classroom.[3] By extension, honors students are presented with opportunities that are becoming increasingly scarce in contemporary higher education.

The benefits associated with honors education have been documented through extant literature, although much of it has been anecdotal in nature given that honors programs and colleges are a relatively understudied aspect of higher education.[4] In 2004, John R. Cosgrove conducted an empirical study that found that "those who complete honors [programs or colleges] have the highest academic performance and graduation rates compared to other high-ability students."[5] The question that should be asked when considering the future of honors education is how educators can provide the benefits to a larger demographic of American undergraduates.

Honors education is executed in two primary forms. The first of which, university-wide honors programs and colleges, recruit incoming freshmen who have shown signs of academic excellence prior to entering higher education. Freshmen are admitted to honors programs and colleges regardless of their chosen major, although the individual institutions set the specific requirements. This type of honors education will be the focus of this chapter. The second form is departmental honors, which provide students the opportunity to engage in advanced scholarly activity within their discipline.

It is incorrect to assume, however, that university-wide honors programs or colleges are homogenous. There are extensive differences in the structure, curriculum, and forms of instruction employed, which many honors scholars believe is a particular strength of honors education.[6] This is founded on the belief that the lack of centralized control encourages honors administrators to tailor their approach to meet the needs of their students. This chapter challenges this notion by asserting that the lack of continuity is having a deleterious effect on honors, as it has prevented the development of a cohesive *honors identity*.

TRAVEL BROADENS THE MIND

Within recent years, the importance of exposing undergraduate students to educational experiences outside of the United States has become solidified. In 2009, R. Michael Paige and colleagues conducted a study that revealed students who studied abroad during their undergraduate career believed it positively impacted their career paths and ability for global engagement.[7] The findings of this study have been reinforced in additional studies, which constantly find that engaging in study abroad programs gives students a deeper understanding of global issues, knowledge and acceptance of other cultures, and increased foreign language skills.[8]

The promotion of study abroad has become increasingly popular in honors programs and colleges across the United States. Honors scholars have focused their attention on the benefits of foreign travel on honors students' intellectual development.[9] According to Rosalie C. Otero, "students who study abroad get a well-rounded education that prepares them for our increasingly global world,"[10] which is a fundamental objective of honors education: exposing honors students to different cultures, languages, and people also enhances their personal and professional growth. Study abroad is subsequently becoming an important part of the honors curriculum.

There has been little scholarly attention given to international models of honors education, especially within the context of how the American model can benefit from examining those approaches. The extant literature that does contribute to this facet of honors education focuses on countries that have been heavily influenced by the American model of honors education. Juan C. Skewes has explored the recent development of honors both within Chile and Latin America, which he believes is "stimulated by experiences in the USA."[11] There has been a similar study focusing on Honduras.[12]

The question posed by this chapter is: How can honors practitioners, administrators, and directors develop and improve honors education in the United States by examining honors models found overseas? Anne N. Rinn pointed out that honors education did not originate in the United States.[13] Approaches to honors education can be found throughout Europe, some of which were established over six hundred years ago. It would therefore be remiss to ignore the lessons that can be learned from these models, most of which have managed to maintain their relevance for centuries.

This chapter considers Scotland, which is home to one of the oldest approaches to honors education in the English-speaking world. The Scottish undergraduate degree of Master of Arts with Honors encompasses a number of the principles associated with honors education in the United States.[14] However, the execution of the program is significantly different, offering interesting insights into ways honors programs and colleges can evolve to meet the challenges of the twenty-first century.

HIGHER EDUCATION IN CONTEXT

Data from the U.S. government indicates that the number of Americans seeking to be admitted to degree-granting institutions continues to increase; between 2002 and 2012, there was a 28 percent rise in the number of full-time students attending U.S. colleges and universities.[15] The expansion has been taking place in concert with colleges and universities making dramatic cuts to their budgets in order to address growing deficits caused by the steady and abrupt removal of state appropriations.

As the student population continues to grow, institutions are finding their resources are strained in ways that can be characterized as unprecedented. This is having a deleterious effect on students' educational experiences through larger class sizes, less teacher-student interaction, and a continued transition away from the principles associated with the Socratic method of pedagogy. Scholars, educators, and commentators continue to stress that if steps are not taken to relieve the strain on resources, it is likely to weaken America's position as a world leader.

University administrators are being forced to consider changes to the American higher education system that will address the challenges it is now facing. Directors of honors programs and colleges are also part of this system-wide discussion, which is taking place at colleges and universities across the United States. It is imperative that these considerations include a debate concerning the form of pedagogy that will ensure that America's next generation of undergraduates continue to receive the world-class education for which American institutions are known.

This chapter deals with the challenges facing higher education and, de facto, honors education by advocating for the expansion of honors education to include a larger demographic of undergraduate students by fighting for the establishment of an honors identity through ensuring greater continuity and oversight of honors programs and colleges and by arguing that the honors community must double down on the relationship between honors education and the liberal arts, which will allow for greater departmental cooperation and increased resources. All of which are characteristics of the Scottish model of honors education.

AN ANCIENT APPROACH TO HONORS

The Scottish model of honors education can be traced back to the early 1400s. Historians have found that the University of St. Andrews first awarded the degree in 1414. The recipient was thirteen-year-old William Yhalulok, who graduated with a Bachelor of Arts in 1413 and then a Master of Arts a year later.[16] Although it might seem strange by today's standards, masters candidates typically began their studies around the age of thirteen and lived under strict supervision from members of the university faculty.

Prior to the 1600s, higher education was something reserved for the aristocracy and those wishing to pursue a career in the Catholic Church. The MA (Hons) curriculum therefore educated candidates in mathematics, literacy, and divinity, which were all considered necessary disciplines for all those entering priesthood. Candidates studied for a period of five years, after which, pending satisfactory completion, they were awarded the title of Master of Arts. Graduates would then enter a compulsory two-year teaching period within the church in order to solidify their competency in the required fields of study.

The success of the MA (Hons) program at the University of St. Andrews resulted in it being expanded to other Scottish universities founded around the same period. The University of Glasgow began offering the program immediately after its founding in 1451, the University of Aberdeen followed in 1495, and finally the University of Edinburgh in 1583.[17] This evolution took place in response to the changing nature of higher education in Scotland, which led into the "Age of Enlightenment" between the 1600s and 1700s.

The Age of Enlightenment fostered an intellectual revolution throughout Western Europe, one particularly influential in Scottish society. During this period there were intellectual and scientific advancements within Scotland, contributing to the founding and development of numerous academic fields, such as philosophy, political science, chemistry, law, economics, and sociology. Scotland has since had ingrained respect for higher education's importance, one that, according to American historian Arthur Herman, "was a springboard for the invention of the contemporary capitalist democracy that now dominates the Western world."[18]

In the late 1700s, the degree began being offered in two distinct parts. Candidates would first complete the ordinary Master of Arts degree, which included tutelage in disciplines associated with the liberal arts.[19] It was stipulated that candidates "attend full courses in at least seven subjects, and shall be examined on all of those subjects."[20] In order to promote a broad and in-depth curriculum, it was also required that "of the subjects, four must be a) Latin or Greek, b) English or modern languages, c) logic and metaphysics or moral philosophy, and d) mathematics and natural philosophy."[21] This became the bedrock of the Scottish model of honors education.

Awarding institutions also recognized the benefits in providing students with the ability to guide their own studies. Having chosen their four compulsory subjects, candidates would select the remaining subjects from an appropriate department, which would determine their *honors group* (or major). The ordinary MA was completed over four or five years, likely due to the age of candidates, some of whom were as young as eleven or twelve.

Candidates who had successfully completed all examinations and paid the required fees would then be conferred the degree of Master of Arts. Graduates would then have the opportunity to request permission to pursue the honors route, which required the candidates to receive instruction in advanced subjects and complete a dissertation in their final year. In order to graduate *with honors*, students would be required to undertake five more years of study, which ensured that only the most capable and dedicated candidates sought the distinction of honors.

Upon successful completion of all requirements, the candidates would be bestowed with the title Master of Arts with Honors, which distinguished graduates who have both an in-depth and broad knowledge of the liberal arts, as well as an advanced specialization in a relevant discipline. In the early twentieth century, the degree evolved to include a system of honors classification. This delineated three *classes of honors*: first, second, and third. This was designed to differentiate MA (Hons) graduates by taking into consideration the quality of submitted work, examination results, and standard of dissertation.

AN ANCIENT DEGREE IN THE TWENTY-FIRST CENTURY

Given its longevity, the MA (Hons) degree can be characterized as being in a constant state of flux, which was imperative in order to maintain its relevance in an ever-changing world. The success of the MA (Hons) program is that the awarding institutions have found a way to execute significant changes without transitioning away from the principles on which the degree was founded. This has ensured that the MA (Hons) continues to prepare undergraduate students for the challenges and demands of their time.

Today, Scotland has fifteen universities; however, the MA (Hons) degree can be awarded only at the five "ancient universities of Scotland," which include the University of St. Andrews, Glasgow, Aberdeen, Edinburgh, and Dundee. The University of Dundee is unique in that it was established in 1967 but is awarded ancient status due to its historical links to the University of St. Andrews. In the words of Sir Graeme Davis, the "Scottish MA (Hons) has been a mark of high quality for centuries."[22] As a result, the ability to award the MA (Hons) degree has long been a sign of exclusivity and quality.

The contemporary MA (Hons) is awarded after four years of full-time study. However, undergraduates can instead choose to graduate with an ordinary Master of Arts after successful completion of their third year of a lower level of specialization. Candidates are required to maintain a high level of academic achievement during years one and two, which are known as the generalization years. In order to progress on to the "honors route," students must maintain a C grade point average in all classes.

The complexities of the modern world have given birth to an array of academic disciplines that seek to explain the myriad facets of the twenty-first century. It is clear that awarding institutions recognize that the MA (Hons) degree is closely associated with the liberal arts. Therefore it has consistently embraced the evolution in academia, including subjects that previously would not have fallen under the rubric of the MA (Hons) degree. This has been achieved without straying from the traditional subjects on which the degree was founded.

MA (Hons) programs are not homogenous, however. The five ancient universities are afforded the right to tailor their program to meet the specific characteristics of the institutions. Variables that influence MA (Hons) programs include, but are not limited to, its size, faculty, students, and mission. This affords prospective undergraduates the opportunity to select an institution that meets their needs and interests, while also presenting them with an honors model that has a strong identity, one that has provided students with quality education for centuries.

The ability to mold one's program to the institution is integral to the success of not only the degree, but also the awarding institutions. If one considers, for a moment, the differences between the University of Dundee and the University of Glasgow: Dundee is a much smaller institution with 10,550 undergraduates, and an annual endowment of $37 million; Glasgow, on the other hand, has 17,000 undergraduate students, and an endowment of $250 million. Given the significant variation in student and financial resources, it makes sense that these two institutions would execute their respective MA (Hons) programs in different ways.

Table 5.1 presents a hypothetical schedule of a MA (Hons) candidate's first and second years pursuing a degree in political science from the University of Dundee. It has been established that candidates must enroll in six courses per academic year, and that four of those six must be in disciplines outside of their "honors groups." This is somewhat unique to other undergraduate degrees offered at nonancient Scottish universities, which results in many first-year students expecting to take only classes connected with their interests and/or declared major.

Table 5.1.   Years one and two of MA (Hons) in political science, University of Dundee

Year One: 2008/2009	Year Two: 2009/2010
PO11001: Politics and Public Policy	AM22002: America: The Land of the Free
PO12001: Political Ideologies	EN21002: Fear and Desire in English Literature
AG1202: The Changing World Order	EU21002: Contemporary Challenges for Europe
EN1001: Introduction to Literary Studies	PI21001: Aesthetics and Kant
EN12004: Approaches to Modern Literature	PO21002: International Relations
PY11001: Introductory Psychology 1	PO22002: Comparative Politics
	EC22002: Macroeconomics and Statistics (Audit)

In the example above, the MA (Hons) candidate's four compulsory classes include PO11011: Politics and Public Policy, PO12001: Political Ideologies, PO21002: International Relations, and PO22002: Comparative Politics. The remaining schedule is made up of courses from a variety of disciplines, including English literature, American studies, psychology, philosophy, and economics. Although the "honors group" department cannot offer electives, students are expected to use their experiences within other disciplines to inform, influence, and enhance their understanding of their own specialization.

Indeed the focus on providing a diverse curriculum is something that is not found in other undergraduate degrees offered at the nonancient universities. This is often daunting for incoming freshmen given that students are required to maintain strong grades throughout the duration of the program. Awarding institutions address these concerns by stipulating that grades acquired during years one and two are not taken into consideration when formulating the candidate's "honors classification." However, high grades are still encouraged in order to be eligible for passage to the honors years.

The Socratic method is used throughout the MA (Hons) degree. However, it is particularly helpful during years one and two because it allows students, the majority of whom are entering from high school, to explore complex topics in an in-depth and comprehensive way. Courses are taught via two one-hour lectures every week. These are conducted alongside a weekly tutorial, made up of ten students or less, that applies the Socratic method to develop and elucidate on the information presented in the lectures.

Presenting students with the opportunity to meet in small groups to discuss and debate important issues with their peers and members of faculty allows them to develop their understanding and hone their interpretation of difficult questions. According to a former lecturer of political science at the University of Dundee, "tutorials are a time when students can develop their own ideas . . . students often find this daunting, apprehensive of the criticism they might receive . . . tutorials are incredibly beneficial to intellectual development."[23]

Table 5.2 depicts the schedule of a MA (Hons) candidate who entered into the honors route and chose to focus within the fields of political science and international relations. The schedule illustrates that the number of required courses decreases from six to four every academic year. These classes utilize the Socratic method to provide candidates with advanced specialization in a narrow academic discipline, which builds upon the broad knowledge acquired during years one and two.

During year four, in order to graduate with honors, students are required to complete a dissertation of no more than 15,000 words in length. The focus of this document must be on an important topic or issue, one that is sufficiently narrow, within their chosen discipline. The dissertation is an opportunity for candidates to bring together their knowledge and methodological training in order to conduct a piece of original research, which contributes to the body of literature within their chosen academic discipline.

Table 5.2. Years three and four of MA (Hons) in political science, University of Dundee

Year Three: 2010/2011	Year Four: 2011/2012
PO31002: Governing the USA	PO40006: Dissertation
PO21002: The Politics of the United Nations	PO41008: Foreign Policy Decision Making
PO32003: The Politics of Transatlantic Relations	PO41002: U.S. Foreign Policy Since 1945
PO32005: Theorizing Politics	PO41009: Russian Politics in Transition

During years three and four, all grades count toward the candidate's final "honors classification" upon successful completion of all other requirements. Depending on the grades achieved throughout the two years, candidates are awarded "first-class," "upper-second-class," "lower-second-class," or "third-class" honors. Those who fail to complete the requirements or do not maintain a sufficient grade point average are awarded their Master of Arts without honors distinction. In the words of Sir Graeme Davis, the "Scottish Master of Arts is not an ordinary undergraduate degree,"[24] and its graduates are held in similar esteem throughout the world.

RECOGNIZING THE NEED FOR CHANGE

Central to the success of the MA (Hons) degree has been its ability to evolve when change is necessary. This is the first hurdle that directors of honors programs and colleges must overcome. There are those within the honors community who are resistant to change, especially change that begins a transition away from honors education as it was originally conceived. Craig T. Cobane puts it succinctly when he opines that "pursuing change within an academic environment can be compared to moving mountains."[25]

The debate that must occur will be both difficult and contentious, but it is one that is absolutely necessary in order for honors education to evolve to meet the needs of the twenty-first century. Universities are facing significant budget deficits, increasing class sizes, and a generation that is becoming increasingly disenfranchised as the cost of undergraduate tuition increases in a world filled with complex challenges. Ensuring that institutions of higher learning continue to provide the next generation with a world-class education has never been more important, and honors must play a more prominent role in American higher education's future.

Directors, practitioners, and advocates of honors programs and colleges must grasp the opportunity to become innovators in American undergraduate education, much like the MA (Hons) embraced its role as the emblem of Scotland's renowned education system during the 1700s. In order for this to succeed, the honors community must unite and embark on a series of significant reforms that will ensure that America continues to produce some of the world's great thinkers and maintain its position as a world leader.

There are three lessons that the honors community can take away from Scotland's ancient model. First, honors education must no longer be the pedagogy for the few, and directors of honors programs and colleges must aspire to offer benefits to a significantly larger demographic of undergraduate students. Second, there must be a concerted effort to establish an "honors identity," one that brings about greater continuity and respect for honors education. Finally, honors programs and colleges must embrace their relationship with other units through promoting integration and collaboration with relevant departments.

THE BROADENING OF HONORS

The concept of honors education began to permeate through the United States at the turn of the twentieth century. At this time scholars were returning from Scottish, English, and German universities, bringing with them methods of instruction not widely known in the majority of American colleges and universities.[26] These included forms of pedagogy that now make up the key tenets of honors education; for example, the Socratic method, tutorial system, and the pass/honors approach in which students receive "pass," "honors," "high honors," or "highest honors."

Honors education, as it is understood today, has existed in the United States since 1922, when Frank Aydelotte established the first honors program at Swarthmore College in Pennsylvania. Aydelotte was a leading advocate of "identifying superior students,"[27] so institutions could ensure that those students were adequately challenged in order to enhance their intellectual development through the use of "honors pedagogy."

Aydelotte's vision for an honors program at Swarthmore College was heavily influenced by the time he spent at Oxford University as a Rhodes Scholar between 1905 and 1907. Robert C. Brooks has postulated that during his time in the United Kingdom, Aydelotte became acquainted with the Oxford methods of instruction, which he believed would greatly enhance American higher education. However, given the elitist nature of English universities, which did not embrace the Scottish universal approach to education, it appears that Aydelotte developed the belief that universities must focus their attention on the "gifted" students on campus.[28]

This vision effectively established a two-tier education system that presents a small group of students with opportunities not available to the wider university community. Aydelotte justified the "elitist" nature of his approach by asserting that "the academic system as ordinar[il]y administered is for these better and more ambitious students a kind of lock step; it holds them back, wastes their time, and blunts their interests."[29] This concept continues to be the underpinning philosophy used to justify the need for honors education.

Many scholars continue to share Aydelotte's vision today, arguing that elitism is an integral part of what constitutes honors, one that must be embraced and continued in order to ensure America's best and brightest minds are properly challenged and nurtured. Honors practitioner Norm Weiner posits that "[honors educators] see honors education as a way to bring benefits like smaller classes and a higher level of intellectual challenge to the best students. . . . Does this make honors education elite? Well, by every definition I can find, yes it does. Selecting the 'choice part or flower . . . of our students . . .' that's what honors is all about."[30]

When advocating this position, Weiner fails to consider the reality of expanding honors to include a larger percentage of undergraduate students because such an evolution would go against the principles that honors education was founded upon. Indeed Weiner elaborates on his position by stating, "While I believe that the benefits we offer . . . should be offered to every college student, the reality is that they aren't."[31] However, given the challenges facing American higher education, should honors educators not give this proposition serious consideration?

Scotland offers a number of notable lessons in this area. Access to honors education is available to all those who have been admitted to a MA (Hons) program at one of the five ancient universities. Given the relative autonomous nature of Scottish universities there is little data concerning the total number of undergraduates enrolling into MA (Hons) programs. However, institutions do publish data on an individual basis; the University of Edinburg enrolled 3,434 students to their MA (Hons) program in the academic year 2012–2013. This equates to an acceptance rate of 10.5 percent, similar to the rates found at America's Ivy League institutions.[32]

The sequence explores a variety of disciplines, including philosophy, history, literature, the arts, and natural, physical, and social sciences. Honors directors and administrators can learn from the MA (Hons) program, which provides all admitted students with the opportunity (in many cases requiring them) to engage with these disciplines during years one and two. Also, honors programs and colleges often implement curriculums that have strict structures, which often limit students' choice. However, the MA (Hons) offers students greater choice in their curriculum with many departments offering multiple courses during the generalization years.

The key difference is that the MA (Hons) degree offers the benefits of honors education—smaller classes, intellectual chal-lenge—to all those who are admitted and chose to enroll in the program. The MA (Hons) program supports the claim made in this chapter that it is indeed possible to expand honors to make it avail-able to a much larger demographic of American undergraduates.

Indeed it is true that implementing such changes brings with it challenges. For example, Scottish universities receive a significant-ly higher percentage of government funding than American institu-tions. Also, the MA (Hons) degree is a philosophical approach to higher education. The Age of Enlightenment ingrained a deep re-spect for the importance of higher education regardless of one's social standing. This influenced the way that Scotland approaches honors education, which believes that all those who are admitted to the same institution and program should have an equal opportunity to benefit from the honors pedagogy.

There is no such tradition in the United States, however, which has approached education in a much more capitalist way than much of Europe. Weiner and others have posited that honors education is beneficial not only as a form of pedagogy for America's brightest students, but also as a recruitment tool for attracting gifted students to institutions that they might otherwise overlook.[33] In the short term, as university administrators are exploring ways to increase student enrolment, it will be difficult to advocate such a significant change. However, doing so will ensure that Americans are not left behind while the United States continues to produce the world's greatest thinkers.

ESTABLISHING AN HONORS IDENTITY

The increasing number of honors programs and colleges speaks to the growing public interest in its unique pedagogical approach to undergraduate education. Honors education is associated with an institution's most talented students, proclaiming that its curriculum is more in depth and challenging compared to what is commonly found on university campuses. However, when asked to describe honors, it is often obvious that students, faculty, and parents find it difficult to articulate a coherent and consistent definition for what constitutes an honors program or college.[34]

In 1994, the National Collegiate Honors Council (NCHC) approved basic characteristics of a fully developed honors program, which attempted to delineate the characteristics that are common to a successful, fully developed honors program. However, in the preamble it is noted that "no one model of an Honors program can be superimposed on . . . institutions."[35] This reinforces the belief held by many within the honors community that the ability of honors programs and colleges to customize their curriculum is pivotal to its success.

In 2010, the NCHC developed and approved basic characteristics of a fully developed honors college in order to provide a sense of clarity given the increasing number of programs and colleges throughout the United States.[36] However, these documents dealt primarily with administrative and functional issues rather than the curriculum, assessments, and forms of pedagogy. These two documents cannot therefore constitute an honors identity because they fail to set any requirements with regard to what is arguably the most important facet of honors education.

There appears to be a contingent within the honors community who believe that the diversity in honors experiences is integral to its mission and, ultimately, success. In the words of Charlie Slavin, honors education "encompasses a wide array of courses, teaching styles, disciplines, and educational objectives."[37] Of course, diversity is important. However, it is time to define what disciplines, pedagogy, and assessments constitute honors education in order to begin establishing and strengthening an honors identity.

The MA (Hons) is an example of how honors programs and colleges can provide students with a diverse curriculum while having a structure that ensures standards and consistency across the country. Indeed it does so without significantly restricting the institution's ability to customize their method. However, implementing a structure of what constitutes honors education would foster unity and confidence among the honors community that all programs and colleges have equivalent methods, curriculum, and goals.

Gregory Lanier states that honors practitioners must promote curricular coherence because the very concept of a "program" or "college" implies that there is a unity and definable focus in the totality of honors education.[38] Lanier eloquently states the difference between honors education and the MA (Hons) degree: the Scottish method of honors education has a structural progression, one that prescribes students expectations in order to compete the process. This ensures that regardless of which institution an MA (Hons) candidate graduates from, they have all received the same level of education, studying similar disciplines and pedagogy of the same quality.

Another example that shows the need of an honors identity is continuity of assessments used to evaluate the quality, progression, and standards of honors students. Assessments within honors programs and colleges are generally insulated from outside influence. These forms of assessment are the responsibility of the honors faculty and director, which, again, means there is little continuity. There also continues to be a lack of external auditing that would ensure that expected standards are being maintained.

Standards are maintained across MA (Hons) programs through the utilization of "external markers."[39] These individuals are made up of professors from both MA (Hons) awarding institutions and nonancient universities from around the world. According to the University of Edinburgh, external markers "must be competent and have the requisite experience to examine the course or programme [*sic*] at the level at which it is taught."[40] This ensures that there is a constant standard across all MA (Hons) institutions, which further strengthens the reputation of the degree, as well as the students who graduate with it.

In order for such oversight to be implemented throughout the honors community, directors of honors programs and colleges must actively seek to develop stronger relationships with fellow institutions. This could be achieved through direct interactions between programs and colleges, or through the NCHC, which must also take a leading role in facilitating such interactions between its members.

The current idiosyncratic nature of honors education makes it inherently difficult to define what constitutes an honors identity. Honors will continue to be disparaged by claims that it is nothing more than a recruitment tool for gifted students, the pedagogy of the elites, and something that only benefits the most gifted students. To establish an honors identity, programs and colleges must strengthen the structure of honors education, ensure oversight of curriculum and assessments, and promote cooperation between programs and colleges—all characteristics of the MA (Hons).

CONCLUDING OBSERVATIONS: DOUBLE DOWN ON THE LIBERAL ARTS AND SCIENCES (?)!

Bruce Kimball once remarked, "Honors programs [and colleges] strive to create the academic experience of a small liberal arts college within a large university."[41] The Association of American Colleges and Universities defines a liberal education as an approach to learning that empowers individuals and prepares them to deal with complexity, diversity, and change. This definition certainly appears to be simpatico with the values and goals of both the Scottish MA (Hons) and honors education in the United States.

The liberal arts have played an important role in the history of both Scotland and the United States. Many university campuses in the United States have a "College of Liberal Arts and Sciences," "School of Liberal Arts," or "Department of Liberal Arts." This is also true of Scotland's ancient universities, as well as other historic universities across Europe. The liberal arts are often considered the intellectual heart of campus, instilling in undergraduates skills that advance intellectual, communicative, and analytical abilities.

In recent years, however, scholars and commentators have written of the "decline of the liberal arts." Arguing that today's students do not seem to value the academic disciplines associated with the liberal arts, instead focusing on high-return subjects like engineering or computer science more likely to land them a lucrative job upon graduation. This is not surprising given the increasing costs associated with receiving an undergraduate education in the United States.

Both honors education and the liberal arts will play leading roles in the future of American higher education and continue to be the foundations of a traditional Scottish education. They offer pedagogical methods that will provide America's future generations with the education they will need to be able to tackle the increasing complexities of the contemporary world. However, in order to ensure the success of honors education and the liberal arts, it is time for significant, difficult, and contentious changes.

Since its conception in 1922, the honors community has been deeply insular, even among its own membership. The time for insularity has now passed. Directors of honors programs and colleges must consider methods outside of their own program or college in order to allow honors education to compete in an evolving education system.

Honors education needs the liberal arts, and the liberal arts needs honors education. At a time when universities are being encouraged to foster and expand "STEM" disciplines, the honors community must be the strongest advocate of colleagues in the liberal arts and a model of education that is broader and more universal than today's standard undergraduate education. In Scotland, the role of ensuring a liberal education is something that is valued by the next generation falls on the Scottish MA (Hons) degree. Through a curriculum developed over centuries, Scotland's ancient universities are ensuring that today's graduates are ready for the challenges of the twenty-first century.

Through briefly examining Scotland's approach to honors education, this chapter has put forward two major changes that would allow honors programs and colleges to serve a much larger role in providing American undergraduates with quality higher education. First, honors must be expanded to include a larger demographic of undergraduate students; the modern world is rendering such elitism redundant and antiquated. Second, the honors community must unite and establish a coherent identity. The idiosyncratic nature of honors has fostered inconsistencies in curriculum, assessment, and quality among programs and colleges. The examination of the Scottish MA (Hons) degree shows that U.S. honors colleges can ensure continuity without losing their ability to provide students with a tailored curriculum, one that meets their students' needs.

In order to ensure that these changes are achievable, honors programs and colleges must seek ways to leverage existing resources within honors and the liberal arts and utilize them in novel ways, which will result in greater funding, resources, and cooperating faculty. Working with, and in some cases incorporating, departments associated with the liberal arts represents an opportunity to combine resources, which, as we have observed in Scotland, allows for the development of a program that meets the needs of all qualified students, ensuring that no gifted, superior, or exceptional student is overlooked.

In a world of dwindling budgets, increased competition, and a global economy, it is important that all students have access to the benefits of an honors education. Although the Scottish MA (Hons) degree does not have all the answers, it is a reminder of what U.S. honors colleges can learn from exploring similar educational models elsewhere in the world.

KEY IDEAS IN THIS CHAPTER

- Research on the internationalization of honors education has thus far focused largely on the export of the American model outward; more research needs to be done on what honors education can learn from similar educational models elsewhere in the world.
- The Scottish MA (Hons) curricular model could be used as a template to ensure greater continuity in curriculum, quality, and experiences across honors programs and colleges.
- In responding to broader societal debates about the value of a liberal arts education, the MA (Hons) model presents an approach to education that is both simultaneously firmly rooted in the liberal arts and provides students with area-specific expertise and skills.

NOTES

1. "Definition of Honors Education," *The National Collegiate Honors Council*, accessed June 2, 2016, http://nchchonors.org/faculty-directors/definition-of-honors-education/.

2. James J. Clauss, "The Benefits of Honors Education for All College Students," *Journal of the National Collegiate Honors Council* 12, no. 2 (2011): 95.

3. Cheryl Achterberg, "What Is an Honors Student?" *Journal of the National Collegiate Honors Council* 6, no. 1 (2005): 77.

4. See, for example, Diane H. Coursol and Edwin E. Wanger, "Prediction of Academic Success in a University Honors Program," *Psychological Review* 58,

no. 1 (1986): 139–142; and Susanna W. Pflaum et al., "The Effects of Honors College Participation on Academic Performance During the Freshman Year," *Journal of College Student Personnel* 26, no. 5 (1985): 414–19.

5. John R. Cosgrove, "The Impact of Honors Programs on Undergraduate Academic Performance, Retention, and Graduation," *Journal of the National Collegiate Honors College* 5, no. 2 (2004): 51.

6. Anthony A. Pittman, "Diversity Issues and Honors Education," *Journal of the National Collegiate Honors College* 1, no. 1 (2001): 135.

7. R. Michael Paige et al., "Study Abroad for Global Engagement: The Long-Term Impact of Mobility Experiences," *Intercultural Education* 20, no. 1 (2009): S29–S44.

8. The literature is voluminous; see, in particular, Jerry S. Carlson et al., *Study Abroad: The Experience of American Undergraduates* (New York: Greenwood Press, 1990); and Philip H. Anderson et al., "Short-Term Study Abroad and Intercultural Sensitivity: A Pilot Study," *International Journal of Intercultural Relations* 30, no. 4 (2006): 457–69.

9. Leena Karsan, Annie Hakim, and Janaan Decker, "Honors in Ghana: How Study Abroad Enriches Students' Lives," *Journal of the National Collegiate Honors Council* 12, no. 1 (2011): 33–36; and Neil Donahue, "The Honors Deferential: At Home and Abroad," *Journal of the National Collegiate Honors Council* 12, no. 1 (2011): 47–50.

10. Rosalie C. Otero, "Faculty-Led International Honors Programs," *Journal of the National Collegiate Honors Council* 12, no. 1 (2011): 45.

11. Juan C. Skewes, "Honors in Chile: New Engagements in the Higher Education System," *Honors in Practice* 59, no. 2 (2006): 16.

12. Trish Folds-Bennett and Marty P. Twomey, "Honors in Honduras: Engaged Learning in Action," *Honors in Practice* 9, no. 3 (2013): 85–98.

13. Anne N. Rinn, "Major Forerunners to Honors Education at the Collegiate Level," *Journal of the National Collegiate Honors Council* 7, no. 2 (2006): 63–84.

14. The ancient Scottish degree of Master of Arts with Honors will be referred to as MA (Hons) throughout the remainder of the chapter.

15. U.S. Department of Education, "National Center for Education Statistics," *Digest of Education Statistics 2013*, chapter 3 (2015).

16. Robert G. Cant, *The University of St Andrews: A Short History* (Edinburgh: Scottish Academic Press, 1970).

17. John Durkan, *The University of Glasgow, 1451–1577* (Glasgow: University of Glasgow Press, 1977).

18. Arthur Herman, *How the Scots Invented the Modern World* (New York: Broadway Books, 2002).

19. The term *liberal arts* traditionally included subjects such as grammar, logic, rhetoric, arithmetic, geometry, music, and astronomy. However, contemporary liberal arts include academic disciplines like philosophy, literature, linguistics, social science, psychology, science, modern languages, and the arts.

20. Scottish Universities Commission, *General Report of the Commissioners: Under the Universities (Scotland) Act, 1889* (Charleston, SC: Nabu Press, 2012), 11.

21. Ibid., 13.

22. Sir Graeme Davis, "Why I Believe the Scottish MA Should be Preserved," *Times Higher Education*, February 4, 2000, accessed October 20, 2014, http://www.timeshighereducation.co.uk/news/why-i-believe-the-scottish-ma -should-be-preserved/150077.article.

23. Author interview with Dr. John MacDonald, August 30, 2014.

24. Sir Graeme David, "Why I Believe," 2000.

25. Craig T. Cobane, "Moving Mountains: Honors as Leverage for Institutional Change," *Journal of the National Collegiate Honors Council* 12, no. 2 (2011): 101.

26. John Seiler Brubacher and Willis Rudy, *Higher Education in Transition: A History of American Colleges and Universities*, fourth edition (New Brunswick, NJ: Transaction Publishers, 2006).

27. Rinn, "Major Forerunners," 64.

28. Robert C. Brooks, *Reading for Honors at Swarthmore: A Record of the First Five Years, 1922–1927* (New York: Oxford University Press, 1927).

29. Frank Aydelotte, *Breaking the Academic Lock Step: The Development of Honors Works in American Colleges and Universities* (New York: Harper and Brother, 1944).

30. Norm Weiner, "Honors Is Elitist, and What's Wrong with That?" *Journal of the National Collegiate Honors Council* 10, no. 1 (2009): 22

31. Ibid., 24.

32. Abby Jackson, "Ivy League Admission Letters Just Went Out—Here Are the Acceptance Rates for the Class of 2020," *Business Insider UK*, April 1, 2016, accessed June 2, 2016, http://uk.businessinsider.com/ivy-league-acceptance -rates-for-the-class-of-2020-2016-3?r=US&IR=T.

33. See Weiner, "Honors Is Elitist"; and Cobane, "Moving Mountains," 2011.

34. Vince Brewton, "What Honors Can Do," *Journal of the National Collegiate Honors Council* 6, no. 1 (2005): 39–42.

35. Peter C. Sederberg, ed., *The Honors College Phenomenon* (Lincoln, NE: National Collegiate Honors Council, 2008).

36. Ibid., 163.

37. Charles Slavin, "Defining Honors Culture," *Journal of the National Collegiate Honors Council* 9, no. 1 (2008): 15–18.

38. Gregory Lanier, "Towards Reliable Honors Assessment," *Journal of the National Collegiate Honors Council* 9, no. 1 (2008): 94.

39. Marc Rands, "The UK Honours Degree Classification System," *The Royal Society of Edinburgh*, December 4, 2004, accessed June 2, 2016, https:// www.royalsoced.org.uk/cms/files/advice-papers/2004/hons_degs.pdf.

40. "University of Aberdeen: Academic Quality Handbook," *The University of Aberdeen*, 2015, accessed June 2, 2016, http://www.abdn.ac.uk/staffnet/ teaching/aqh/section9.pdf.

41. Bruce Kimball, "Revising the Declension Narrative: Liberal Arts Colleges, Universities, and Honors Programs, 1870s–2010s," *Harvard Educational Review* 84, no. 2 (2014): 243–64.

Chapter Six

Across the Great Divide

Distance Education and the Future of Honors

Robert W. Glover and Katherine M. O'Flaherty

Defining honors education is no simple task. Yet if one were to review the mission statements of honors programs and colleges, providing opportunities for face-to-face, personalized intellectual exchange between students and faculty would be nearly universal.

The National Collegiate Honors Council states that honors education is predicated on "the belief that superior students profit from close contact with faculty, small courses, seminars or one-on-one instruction" and that the "*essence* of honors education is personalized attention."[1] Yet in a future likely to be increasingly shaped by technology, honors educators face a problematic challenge that seems to test the human interaction deemed central to honors education.

Michael Moore and Greg Kearsley define distance education as "teaching and planned learning in which teaching normally occurs in a different place from learning, requiring communication through technologies as well as special institutional organization."[2] The most prevalent way in which teaching and learning have become unbundled is via online education where, by design, teaching and learning are separated spatially (and quite often temporally).

For the purposes of this chapter, distance education is used as defined here, with the understanding that online education constitutes one such type of distance education.

The lack of honors education scholarship on distance education reflects a relative unwillingness, thus far, to consider the compatibility of the two. Over ten years ago, Jon A. Schlenker argued that "those colleges and universities that desire or need to present their honors courses and programs to students at a distance are only limited by their resources (human and financial), creativity, and imagination."[3] While online course management software is now ubiquitous in many honors courses, honors educators have generally been reluctant to think about more expansive and demanding modes of distance education.

Paradoxically, despite claims to foster independent learning and self-praise for pedagogical innovation, honors often continues to be an environment in which many educators view teaching and learning as tightly bound together, both temporally and spatially. This at least in part explains the general reluctance to consider educational modalities that might displace traditional models of discussion-based learning or face-to-face mentorship.

As one recent commentary noted, "rarely . . . have honors educators discussed how honors programs and colleges can embrace digital initiatives that go beyond preserving small-class, individualized experiences, especially if these initiatives seem to threaten traditional honors experiences."[4] For many, the push toward distance education is *antithetical* to honors education; the two simply cannot coexist, for to pursue distance education, through online or hybrid teaching, would be to undermine and obliterate what makes honors education valuable.

These fears can extend to technology generally. For instance, in a recent special issue of the *Journal of the National Collegiate Honors Council* dedicated to "Honors in a Digital Age," Richard Badenhausen expressed fears that "digital technologies often cultivate passivity, lack of awareness of the larger world, and the type of cocoon-like isolation that honors education attempts to overcome."[5]

This sentiment is widespread; many educators view the honors classroom as a "sanctuary" or "refuge" from the heavily mediatized environment of gadgetry and digital communications devices, a place where students might pause and critically reflect.[6] However, this position may be unnecessarily absolute. A more productive way forward might be to consider what dimensions of technology, and more specifically delivery options to facilitate distance learning, could be adapted to fit an honors model, and what this might look like in practice.

The stakes of initiating this conversation could not be higher. Honors educators can ill afford to think of distance education as something in which they simply do not engage. Shifting elements of the curriculum online is frequently touted as providing important savings in terms of *cost*, at a time when many administrators are making difficult decisions in a context of severe budgetary constraints.

Additionally, there are related considerations with regard to *equity* and *access* (addressed elsewhere in this edited series). The reality of higher education in the United States is that less affluent and advantaged groups are unlikely to be able to partake in a traditional "liberal arts college" educational experience and may have lives and commitments that make distance education more suitable for their needs. To simply dismiss the notion that portions of the honors experience can be translated to the more flexible and accessible format risks saying that these opportunities are simply not available to them.

Lastly, there are implications with regard to *quality*. Distance education is a rapidly growing enterprise and honors education is a field recognized to provide "value added" to an educational degree. If those engaged in traditional classroom-based honors education do not think seriously and proactively about what elements of the honors experience are scalable and adaptable to distance educational frameworks, some other entity may do so and honors educators might not like the result.

This chapter aims to think systematically about distance education and honors, utilizing insights from innovations in community engagement, defined as "collaboration between institutions of higher education and their larger communities (local, regional/state, national, global) for the mutually beneficial exchange of knowledge and resources in a context of partnership and reciprocity."[7]

Within this broad educational movement, those who have sought to embed learning in the community have faced similar challenges—claims that online and hybrid learning modalities are antithetical to the type of engaged, experiential activity they view as the hallmark of high-impact learning. However, increasingly, these challenges are faced head-on, often with surprisingly effective results.

As Dan W. Butin notes, the rise of distance education has provided those involved in community engagement with "a precipitous moment where traditional models and norms no longer apply so easily or thoroughly . . . an opportunity that could lead us to new and better modes of engaging and improving our communities."[8]

What can honors educators learn from these pioneering attempts to adapt community engagement to an online setting? What parallels exist between these efforts and those faced in honors education? What trade-offs are honors educators making when they shift portions of the honors experience online? Are the changes acceptable, educationally and ethically?

While it is unlikely that one could ever envision honors education conducted completely through a distance learning framework, or see the moment of teaching and learning unbundled for the entirety of the honors experience, these new learning modalities might offer a chance to think creatively about honors' collective future.

ENGAGEMENT AND SERVICE LEARNING IN HIGHER EDUCATION

Educators are currently in the midst of an "engagement turn" in higher education. The notion that American colleges and universities have a broader public mission has a long history, dating to the creation of land grant institutions in the mid-nineteenth century and earlier.[9] Educational philosopher John Dewey emphasized the importance of learning by doing and instilling a sense of community responsibility in his articulation of "progressive education" in the early twentieth century.[10]

A variety of campus-based service programs emerged and thrived throughout the latter half of the twentieth century, while research universities concurrently developed ever stronger ties with the federal government to serve as hubs for advanced scientific research.[11] However, the timing of this most recent rise in community engagement roughly parallels the proliferation of honors education in the United States, outlined in the opening chapters of this volume.

As Ira Harkavy and Rita Axelroth Hodges note,

> since the end of the Cold War, there has been a substantive and public re-emergence of engaged scholarship. Leading academics and university presidents have made the intellectual case that higher education institutions, particularly urban universities, would better fulfill their core academic functions, including advancing knowledge and learning, if they focused on improving conditions in their cities and local communities.[12]

Community engagement is a broad term that captures a wide range of activities that straddle the traditional academic boundaries of research, service, and teaching.[13] With respect to pedagogy, those at the forefront of the "engagement turn" have sought to link the missions of their courses and craft their curricula in alignment with concerns, questions, and challenges emanating in the community.

Deemed "service learning," such courses combine service to the community with instruction and reflection in an effort to enhance the learning experience, foster a sense of community responsibility, and directly impact and benefit the communities themselves.

Service-learning courses have taken shape in a variety of different ways across a range of different academic disciplines and programs. Such courses generally involve a community project or activity that in some way blends academic learning with hands-on experience. Examples abound.

Students in a graduate-level grant writing class might partner with local nonprofit organizations to enhance the entity's grant-seeking capacity and gain hands-on experience. Students in an upper-level history course might partner with a local library to conduct oral histories and assist in their curation. Nursing students might partner with local K–12 schools to lead workshops and activities educating younger students about dimensions of health and wellness.

In the social sciences, students could partner with local municipal governments and nonprofits to co-design and co-execute policy research projects on community concerns and challenges. Yet all of these activities would be carried out with forethought, intentional design, and reflection designed to help students gain a broader appreciation of course content.

Beyond their potential benefit to the community, service-learning courses promise tangible gains in terms of student educational outcomes. There are a range of potential benefits: improved student learning broadly congruent with findings from other active learning techniques, the tangible skills gained through collaboration on real-world projects, fostering a sense of community among students, and the acquisition of analytical and critical thinking skills.[14] Beneficial impacts can also include personal growth and development, including increased moral awareness or the enhancement of leadership skills. [15]

The annual National Survey of Student Engagement (NSSE) includes service-learning courses as one of its "high impact educational practices" experiences closely correlated with desirable learning gains and overall educational satisfaction. [16]

In many senses, community engagement and service learning bear certain structural similarities to honors. Engaged approaches do not constitute a field of study or a "discipline" in and of themselves. Rather, they constitute a lens or framework through which students and educators structure their inquiry.

From an institutional standpoint, both honors and community engagement constitute a way of providing "value added" to traditional degree programs. They build upon the existing academic experience to offer opportunities and growth experiences for a subset of high-achieving students. Thus it is no coincidence that the opportunities and advantages associated with both honors and engagement figure prominently in higher education recruitment efforts.

Honors and community engagement also share structural similarities in terms of their challenges. Both approaches to higher education are potentially time consuming and labor intensive for students and educators. These pedagogical settings require self-directed, motivated learning on behalf of students.

In addition, both honors and community engagement entail a loss of control for the instructor. In honors, faculty must be willing to cede some degree of control over the direction of class conversations and to allow students autonomy in the selection of research and creative projects. In community engagement and service learning, collaborating with community partners in authentic, reciprocal ways requires flexibility and faculty willingness to share authority over the direction of the collaboration with community partners and the students themselves.

DISTANCE EDUCATION AND SERVICE LEARNING

As noted earlier, service learning seems at first glance to be a problematic fit for distance education. In these courses, faculty find themselves navigating the needs and demands of multiple constituencies, fostering and facilitating partnerships that produce meaningful benefit not only for the students, but also for community entities. Doing so absent regular face-to-face interaction would seem to make an already challenging pedagogical framework next to impossible.

How would such a commitment to meaningful collaboration emerge absent the opportunity for the relevant parties to engage face-to-face, building trust and carefully addressing challenges and complications as they emerge? Yet in another sense, there are ways in which service learning is uniquely positioned to take full advantage of the potential benefits of distance education, perhaps more so than classes that do not have an engaged service-learning component.

As noted at the outset, the hallmark of distance education is the separation or "unbundling" of teaching and learning. It is inherent in the design of distance education offerings that the space of teaching and the space of learning are separated by geographical distance and, quite often, time (that is, asynchronous learning environments in which students access and digest course content at their own pace).

Technology of various kinds serves as the mechanism that makes this unbundling possible. Online education utilizes project management applications, message boards, podcasts, video conferencing, chat rooms, wikis, blogging, and so on. Before this, distance learning used more rudimentary technologies such as mail correspondence or interactive television (ITV) to structure distance learning, but the principle was essentially the same. [17]

The instructor in a distance education environment almost by definition cannot adopt the "sage on a stage" model of direct transmission of knowledge. Rather, their role is to provide participants with conceptual knowledge and analytical tools, while designing interactive settings in which students deploy these tools for maximum educational impact.

Here one notices certain fundamental similarities that distance learning shares with community engagement and service learning. Educators that adopt service learning are providing conceptual knowledge and analytical tools that will then be put to use in community settings, with the hope of addressing some fundamental community need. Faculty may structure the way in which students interact in the community, as well as the knowledge and skills they bring into the community setting, but perhaps the most important knowledge acquisition and learning will occur in spaces outside of the instructor's control; they may not even be present.

The experience-based and practical insights gained in these settings are reinforced through the practice of reflection, an essential dimension of service learning. As Robert G. Bringle and Julie A. Hatcher note, "when reflection activities engage the learner in dialogue with other forms of communication about the relationship between relevant, meaningful service and the interpretative template of a discipline, there is enormous potential for learning to broaden and deepen along academic, social moral, and civic dimensions." [18] Thus even when conducted live, service learning accepts that learning will occur separate from the classroom.

Somewhat unsurprisingly then, innovators in higher education have undertaken the effort to envision and execute service learning in distance learning settings for over a decade. These experiments vary in terms of the content of the courses, as well as the ambitiousness of the collaborations they undertake. Yet despite such diversity one can think of ways to map such efforts. Specifically, educators can think of distance service learning operating along a continuum with two basic axes: 1) the scale of the project and 2) the extent to which the experience is structured via distance learning (represented as the x and y axes in figure 6.1).

Setting aside factors such as academic discipline, or whether the course is upper level or introductory, these are the key dimensions in which educators can think about a service-learning experience structured via distance education. At one end, one can imagine a very limited foray into distance education and service learning that uses a "hybrid" blend of distance learning platforms in the context of a traditional classroom-based course. This could perhaps be a single volunteer experience in which parts of the postservice "reflection" are posted via a class message board or blog, a "digital inflection," as opposed to in person.

At the other end of this dual continuum, one could imagine an expansive project in terms of its scope and duration, occurring in a fully distance learning setting (that is, both the class *and* the service

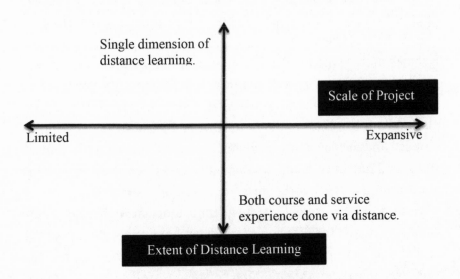

Figure 6.1.   Conceptually Mapping Distance and Service-Learning Design. Source: Original contribution by chapter authors.

experience are conducted without traditional face-to-face contact). This latter experience is sometimes referred to as "extreme e-service."[19] For instance, Leora S. Waldner and co-authors described an "extreme e-service" experience in an online graduate course where students collaborated with a nonprofit organization to develop a full marketing plan for the organization as well as strategies for promotion of organizational objectives and events.[20]

Returning to the definition of distance learning—a separation of the spaces in which learning and teaching occur—one can think of the y axis as the extent of this separation. The greater the extent of this separation, the more advance planning and organization must occur, and the more the students themselves shape and control the learning experience. Yet the separation itself does not mean that service learning is not feasible.

The variety of ways in which distance and service learning, two seemingly disparate pedagogies, have been combined and the successful and interesting ways that they can fruitfully coexist is nothing short of remarkable. Across higher education, there is a growing recognition that service learning can be successful in a distance learning setting, and the technologies associated with distance learning can actually be a tool to embark upon service-learning projects with a broader geographical reach and a more diverse pool of students.

As Kathy L. Guthrie and Holly McCracken write, "instruction in the virtual classroom, when coupled with on-site service experiences, creates opportunities for a unique combination of learning activities constructed to be individually and collectively relevant and focused on real-world problems."[21] In fact, in "extreme service learning" scenarios, one might go even further to say that service can be construed even more broadly than "on-site" service experiences.

In certain types of courses, this could greatly enrich the experiences that form the basis of reflection as students tackle diverse issues in different cultural and societal contexts, or step beyond the types of experiences available to them in their immediate locale. In the next section, the focus turns to what has been learned from these experiences before applying the insights to distance education within an honors context.

WHAT HAS BEEN LEARNED

The "meta-insight" that emerges from efforts to integrate distance and service learning is that there is no inherent conflict between the two frameworks. The two can coexist and can do so relatively well, provided that they are combined with care and foresight. But what exactly does this mean? There are a variety of ways in which one can parse out the meaning of "care" and "forethought."

Technology

The dominant framework for facilitating distance learning is currently through online or hybrid courses that blend online and classroom learning. Thus it is through the use of technology that educators connect students with content, provide access to faculty and peers, and perhaps even to the community partners with whom they will work in service-learning experiences in the case of "extreme e-service" courses.

Honors educators are reliant and dependent on technology, meaning they must ensure that a) all parties utilizing the technology have adequate understanding of how it works and b) provide professional development and training for those individuals (be they students, faculty, or support staff) whose competencies and skills are lacking.[22] In addition, educators must be aware that there will be glitches that could not have possibly been foreseen that will force adjustments to curricular plans. Flexibility and patience are virtues necessary when dealing with any technology, but this is particularly true with regard to distance learning.[23]

Furthermore, as distance learning has grown and evolved, service-learning educators have stressed the value in "starting small."[24] Service learning has grown through incremental, deliberate integration into distance learning frameworks. Educators can begin with limited objectives that present few technological or logistical challenges and scale aspirations upward as these are successfully integrated into the distance education framework.

Course Design

With regard to course design, a key insight is that one ought not simply attempt to replicate the experiences of the classroom in an online setting. In most service-learning courses, this would simply be impossible. Geographical dispersal of students in an online setting might force an instructor to be more flexible with the types of service experiences in which the students will engage, for example. Reflection exercises that might normally be done in face-to-face discussion might have to be conducted via a blog or message board.

Beyond this, numerous scholars have pointed out that effective online course design involves more than content delivery and assessment of student comprehension. Distance education involves creating spaces for student interaction and the motivation and comfort to do so. Simone C. O. Conceição and Chip Donahue write that the most effective online educators utilize online teaching methods "that encourage interaction, establish presence for instructors and students, and motivate students to participate in an in-depth, convenient, and flexible environment in which they have control over the learning process."[25]

These methods are geared toward a different educational experience altogether, in which the learners operate as the effective "center" of the experience. Moore and Kearsley go so far as to suggest that this constitutes a "Copernican revolution" for higher education, in that the learners now constitute the "center of the universe."[26] They write that "students must accept the consequence of assuming more responsibility for managing their own learning, in such matters as deciding when they will study, how much they want to learn, and seeking out information and resources."[27]

In addition, the instructor must design the course activities and the types of interactions in which the students will engage with a clear sense of how they will relate to and reinforce overarching course learning objectives. A distance learning course in which those objectives are not clearly defined and the linkages between course content and activities and objectives is not adequately laid out might end up being a frustrating experience for educator and students alike.

ASSESSMENT AND FEEDBACK

In service learning, assessment and data collection are extremely important. A broad consensus exists among service-learning practitioners that the key to vital information regarding student learning outcomes, community partner satisfaction, and sustainability of partnerships is timely collection of relevant information. Doing this effectively involves in part the clear communication of realistic expectations to all parties involved in advance of the service-learning experience. The instructor might even formalize this through the use of a "memorandum of understanding" or a "service-learning contract."

Beyond this, however, it involves the construction of assessment metrics, administered periodically to determine whether participant needs are being met and to gather feedback about what would be improved. In a distance learning setting, this is even more essential. The instructor in this setting by definition will have less direct contact and interaction with participants in the course.

Traditional end-of-semester course evaluations will be inadequate to determine what is going well and what is in need of change. These are likely not designed with a service-learning experience in mind, and even if they were, the feedback will arrive too late to adapt to issues as they emerge. Institutions must gather data at multiple points throughout the experience, constructing formative rather than summative assessments of course success. While these insights are true of courses generally, they are crucial for service learning in distance education settings.

Cultural Considerations

One final note on what researchers have learned taps into the ethical dimensions in the shift toward distance learning, much of it mediated by computers and online technology. Guthrie and McCracken remind us that "computers are not culturally neutral but amplify the characteristics of those who design, promote, and use them."[28] The essential point being made here is that no technological medium operates neutrally, absent a value structure.

Service learning in particular takes concerns about social justice and inequality seriously. Educators must be attentive not only to concerns regarding skill level and competency, but also to the role that technologies can play in affirming existing inequalities embedded within the societal status quo. In the most immediate sense, this occurs with the problematic assumption that students somehow transcend socioeconomic status and the technology necessary for such courses is ubiquitous. This is not always the case, particularly in more socioeconomically diverse student bodies.

Educators must be mindful that contemporary inequalities are stark, resulting in variability in access and ease of use for digital technologies. Beyond this, there is a problematic tendency within distance education to market and package learning as merely another commodity (in much the same way that one now uses online delivery systems to consume entertainment, sex, social interaction, and so on). This is a more challenging cultural tendency to resist, but educators must push against that problematic trend in any way possible.

ONLINE EDUCATION AND HONORS

Thus with service learning honors educators encounter a pedagogical framework seemingly an ill fit for distance education that nevertheless can find ways to use these perceived weaknesses as strengths. The question remains: What might educators in honors take as insights as they ponder whether and how to incorporate distance education into the distinctive educational frameworks?

One might begin with a couple of important caveats. The first is that it is unlikely that the *entirety* of an honors experience should ever be shifted to a distance education model for three reasons. First, the faculty in many honors colleges and programs would be understandably resistant. Honors faculty typically have less stringent research expectations than traditional faculty positions and a higher percentage of their work involves dealing directly with students. They would be reluctant to see this replaced by distance learning entirely, and without faculty support such a model could never work.

Second, the faculty structure in many honors programs and colleges is simply too diverse and heterogeneous at the moment for it to make institutional sense to invest in the professional development and training necessary to do distance learning well. While tenure stream and permanent faculty models specific to honors are beginning to emerge, the majority of honors faculty are in more contingent roles: faculty from other departments teaching in honors in an overload capacity, fully or partially retired faculty, lecturers on continuing reappointment, or adjunct faculty.

To invest significant time and resources developing capacity for faculty who are not contractually bound to continue teaching in honors could prove quite problematic. Significant time, energy, and resources could be spent training faculty for a challenging pedagogical model with nothing preventing those individuals from moving on. For this to make sense, structural changes in the honors faculty model may have to come first.

Third, an honors model rooted fully in distance learning would be problematic for students. Honors students typically need the most attention at the outset of the honors experience (as they are socialized to honors education and its expectations) and its close (as they complete their thesis or culminating project). The learner-centric model of distance education places demands upon students they may be ill prepared to meet at either stage of their educational careers.

Course Content: Efficiency and Expansion

Nevertheless, one can envision ways in which elements of distance learning could be implemented into existing honors curricula incrementally. For instance, distance learning (particularly hybrid models) could be an exciting way in which honors educators think about more efficient content delivery in honors courses. For instance, many honors colleges and programs have discussion-based topical seminars and tutorials for students in the middle third of the curriculum. Faculty might feel torn between the competing demands of providing needed context to situate the course material and devoting adequate time to student-centered, discussion-based learning.

Here faculty could essentially utilize a "flipped" classroom model, hosting podcasts, lectures, media content, and primary source materials through online course management software so less contextualization need be provided by the instructor within the classroom. This also means that students become responsible for their own learning in a way that they might not be in more traditional models of content delivery.

Alternatively, online message boards and blogs could be used as a setting in which additional discussion and inquiry can continue outside of the classroom setting. This additionally provides students who are hesitant to speak up in small group discussions or who take longer to mull over ideas and formulate their thoughts a venue in which they can share their perspectives.

Beyond this, one could envision a distance education model being used for seminars that focus more on "process" than content. For instance, it is fairly common to have honors seminars focusing on basic research skills or the process of writing the thesis itself. Some honors colleges and programs might be hard-pressed to make such an offering available to *all* of their students and it exists instead as an optional course offering that only some students will take.

Delivering such courses partially or fully via distance learning could expand the potential opportunities to take this course. In addition, it might make it possible to teach the course in the "off season," that is, as a winter or summer session course. It is rare to have honors course offerings beyond the traditional semester system. However, utilizing distance learning could make such offerings possible.

Harnessing the Power of Geographic Dispersal

Distance learning by definition implies geographic dispersal. While this might be viewed as a potential challenge or obstacle to student-centered learning, it can be harnessed as a means to enhance the learning experience for students. For instance, due to GPA requirements for most study abroad programs, students in honors are a higher percentage of the student body participating in study abroad experiences than the student body as a whole. Some honors programs and colleges even mandate such an experience. Thus at any given time an honors college or program might have a number of students dispersed in various locales globally.

Distance education provides online settings in which students who are spatially dispersed, even on a global scale, can share experiences and engage in reflection about the continuity and discontinuity in their experiences. These courses could be structured in ways that wed the experience abroad to the questions and themes engaged in these students' home institutions.

Distance educational platforms could also enable thematically organized collaborative courses taught across institutions. Online platforms could enable students studying at different institutions with different geographies, cultures, student profiles, and socioeconomic profiles to engage around a shared theme and curriculum. Intentionality and advance planning around this collaboration would be essential.

Yet a variety of potential focal points could be envisioned. For instance, colleges and programs in two different locations could examine immigration along two different borders, poverty in rural versus urban settings, or through international collaboration, two groups of students could examine the impacts of climate change in two very different societies and geographic locations. Such possibilities for collaboration are intellectually exciting and might encourage faculty who are a bit skeptical of distance learning to consider partaking in these offerings.

LESSONS FOR HONORS

The potential opportunities to integrate distance education, as well as the scale and specifics of such efforts, will vary from institution to institution. Yet honors educators can speak of shared considerations that such institutions should take into account as they think about how distance education can map on to their existing efforts.

1. The shift to distance education cannot be done simply for budgetary reasons.

As noted at the outset, one of the key reasons deans and administrators might face an increasing push to consider distance education is budgetary. Yet what must be resisted at all costs are haphazard and sloppy efforts to push elements of the honors curriculum online for perceived line item savings. To successfully launch such efforts, institutions will likely have to make significant initial in-vestments in faculty and staff development, technical support, and equipment.

Additionally, as often occurs with service-learning efforts, insti-tutions will likely need to incentivize faculty to get involved in such an effort, providing material support to help faculty shift from more familiar learning models to something entirely new. These efforts *may* ultimately enable institutions to save money by ena-bling broader content delivery. However, if institutions make this transition with a singular goal of cost savings, they might not pro-vide the resources necessary to make these innovations successful in the long term.

2. Institutions must recognize and prepare for the ways in which distance education will mean a loss of control for faculty.

One of the hardest points of transition for faculty moving into service learning is the loss of control over the various elements of the educational experience. Particularly for long-term service-learning projects, there are a variety of elements that remain outside of the instructor's control: variability in student reflection, chang-ing community partner needs, unforeseen delays or challenges, and so on.

The simple fact is that the learning environment in a traditional classroom will always enable a greater degree of faculty control. The same is true for distance learning. This means that distance learning will *not* be for everyone, and faculty cannot be forced into a model with which they have deep misgivings. It also means that the micro-grants and professional development will be important in preparing faculty for an experience that might be a source of anxie-ty.

3. While distance education may make sense for certain types of experiences, it could be disastrous for others. It makes sense to "start small" and proceed in incremental steps.

As noted earlier, each institution's needs and capacities will be different. However, honors colleges and programs should approach any transition to distance learning with intentionality. Distance learning likely cannot be the educational framework used for all aspects of the honors experience.

It is likely that traditional classroom experiences or face-to-face mentoring should "bookend" the honors experience when the students' need for direction and regular faculty interaction will be most acute. Each institution must think carefully about what would work in a distance setting and what might not. And like service learning, it will make sense for institutions to "start small" and gradually scale up their distance education efforts.

4. Assessment is essential and should be built into the distance education experience prior to its commencement.

All distance education efforts involve attending systematically to assessment. Honors will be no exception. Ensuring that the honors experience is not being devalued or diminished by shifting elements of the curriculum online will force institutions to think about both programmatic and curricular goals and ways that these might be measured. To ensure quality, institutions must build in methods to assess their distance education efforts from the outset of this transition.

This extends beyond merely efforts targeted at students to faculty and support staff and these efforts can integrate both qualitative and quantitative assessment. These data can be maintained over time and periodically reviewed longitudinally, informing subsequent efforts in terms of curricular design, professional development, and training.

CONCLUSION

At the outset, this chapter raised some of the general fears that accompany distance learning and honors education, as well as the technology often used to deliver it. Honors educators are right to raise these questions. Distance learning implies not only logistical and institutional challenges, but also ethical challenges.

Honors educators are right to think carefully about resisting the temptations to fuse education with the latest technological innovation. Honors' distinctiveness lies partly in its penchant for innovation and exploration, but perhaps more so in its reverence for the past—of reading important texts and attending to the enduring questions that have shaped the human experience. Programmatic and curricular innovation that could potentially change this have ethical implications that should shape and inform decisions made by institutions.

Yet at the same time, honors cannot be a cloistered intellectual enclave that resists changes and innovations simply because they are different or unfamiliar. This too would run fundamentally against the grain of honors education. While distance education requires honors educators to think about the honors experience in new ways, one should view this as an opportunity to thoughtfully consider possibilities for growth and change in honors.

Honors' relative strength, and the way that it might continue to provide "value added" to higher education, lies not in resistance to distance education altogether, but rather the possibility that efforts can open up even more possibilities for student growth and exploration utilizing the new tools at our disposal.

KEY IDEAS IN THIS CHAPTER

- In a future increasingly shaped by technology, honors educators must grapple with the compatibility of online-based distance learning and honors education.
- Because honors educators continue to see learning as tightly bound to teaching, more research specific to honors and distance learning is necessary.

- The entirety of an honors education should likely not be moved to an online model because of faculty resistance, heterogeneity of position structure, and a variety of student needs, yet incremental integration of distance learning could actually enhance the honors experience.

- Attending to concerns about equity in honors education may mean adjusting our expectations regarding the format and design of the learning experience, potentially drawing upon distance learning to attend to these concerns.

NOTES

1. "What Is Honors?" accessed May 28, 2014, http://nchchonors.org/public-press/what-is-honors/.

2. Michael Moore and Greg Kearsley, *Distance Education: A Systems View of Online Learning*, third edition (Belmont, CA: Wadsworth, 2012), 12.

3. Jon A. Schlenker, "Technology, Distance Education, and Honors," *Journal of the National Collegiate Honors Council* 3, no. 2 (2002): 21.

4. Elizabeth Nix, Brian Etheridge, and Paul Walsh, "A Traditional Educational Practice Adapted for the Digital Age," *Honors in Practice* 10 (2014): 41.

5. Richard Badenhausen, "Immigrant Song: A Cautionary Note about Technology in Honors," *Journal of the National Collegiate Honors Council* 10, no. 2 (2009): 30.

6. Badenhausen, "Immigrant Song"; Scott Carnicom, "Honors Education: Innovation or Conservation?" *Journal of the National Collegiate Honors Council* 12, no. 2 (2011): 49–54; Dail Mullins, "The Times They Are a Changin'," *Journal of the National Collegiate Honors Council* 9, no. 1 (2008): 41–44; Emily Walshe, "Postmodern Prometheans: Academic Libraries, Information Technologies, and the Cut-and-Paste Aesthetic," *Journal of the National Collegiate Honors Council* 10, no. 2 (2009): 23–27.

7. Carnegie Foundation for the Advancement of Teaching, "Community Engagement Elective Classification," accessed June 20, 2014, http://classifications.carnegiefoundation.org/descriptions/community_engagement.php?utm_source=Carnegie+Foundation+Mailing+List&utm_campaign=3b5562162a-CE_Classification_announcement_2013&utm_medium=emai.

8. Dan W. Butin, "Does Community Engagement Have a Place in a Placeless University?" *New England Board of Higher Education*, accessed May 28, 2014, http://www.nebhe.org/thejournal/ moocs-will-save-us-or-not-does-community-engagement-have-a-place-in-a-placeless-university/.

9. Lee Benson, Ira Harkavy, and John Puckett, *Dewey's Dream: Universities and Democracies in an Age of Education Reform: Civic Society, Public Schools, and Democratic Citizenship,* (Philadelphia, PA: Temple University Press, 2007); Linda Silka et al., "Moving Beyond the Single Discipline: Building a Scholarship of Engagement that Permeates Higher Education," *TAMARA: Journal for Critical Organizational Inquiry* 11, no. 4 (2013): 41–52.

10. John Dewey, *Democracy and Education* (New York: Simon and Schuster, 1916).

11. Barbara Jacoby, "Civic Engagement in Today's Higher Education: An Overview," in *Civic Engagement and Higher Education: Concepts and Practices,* ed. Barbara Jacoby (San Francisco, CA: Jossey Bass, 2009), 11–12.

12. Ira Harkavy and Rita Axelroth Hodges, "Democratic Devolution: How America's Colleges and Universities Can Strengthen Their Communities," *Progressive Policy Institute,* 2012, accessed June 20, 2014, http://www.compact.org/wp-content/uploads/2009/01/Democratic-Devolution-How-Americas-Colleges-and-Universities-Can-Strengthen-Their-Communities.pdf, 3–4.

13. Amy Driscoll, "Carnegie's Community Engagement Classification: Affirming Higher Education's Role in the Community," *New Directions in Higher Education* 147 (2009): 5–12.

14. Alexander W. Astin et al., "How Service Learning Affects Students," *Higher Education Research Institute,* accessed June 19, 2014, http://heri.ucla.edu/pdfs/rhowas.pdf; Janet E. Eyler and Dwight E. Giles, *Where's the Learning in Service-Learning?* (San Francisco, CA: Jossey Bass, 1999); David J. Hagenbuch, "Service Learning Inputs and Outcomes in a Personal Selling Course," *Journal of Marketing Education* 28, no. 1 (2006): 26–34; Sarena D. Siefer and Kara Connors, "Faculty Toolkit for Service-Learning in Higher Education," *Learn and Serve America's National Service-Learning Clearinghouse,* 2007, accessed June 20, 2014, http://ccph.memberclicks.net/assets/Documents/FocusAreas/he_toolkit.pdf; J. Lynn McBrien, "The World at America's Doorstep: Service Learning in Preparation to Teach Global Students," *The Journal of Transformative Education* 6, no. 4 (2008): 270–85.

15. Janet E. Eyler et al., *At A Glance: What We Know about The Effects of Service-Learning on College Students, Faculty, Institutions and Communities, 1993–2000,* third edition, accessed June 6, 2014, http://ewucommunityengagement.pbworks.com/w/file/fetch/62951195/aag.pdf; James A. Ejiwale, "Leadership Skills Development Through Service Learning," Proceedings of the 2008 Midwest Section Conference of the American Society for Engineering Education, accessed June 12, 2014, https://www.asee.org/documents/sections/midwest/2008/101-3.pdf.

16. National Survey of Student Engagement, *A Fresh Look at Student Engagement: Annual Results 2013* (Bloomington, IN: Indiana University Center for Postsecondary Research, 2013), accessed June 20, 2014, http://nsse.iub.edu/NSSE_2013_Results/pdf/NSSE_2013_Annual_ Results.pdf.

17. Moore and Kearsley, *Distance Education,* 3.

18. Robert G. Bringle and Julie A. Hatcher, "Reflection in Service Learning: Making Meaning of Experience," in *Introduction to Service-Learning Toolkit: Readings and Resources for Faculty*, second edition (Boston: Campus Compact, 2003), 84.

19. Leora S. Waldner, Sue Y. McGorry, and Murray C. Widener, "Extreme E-Service Learning (XE-SL): E-Service Learning in the 100% Online Course," *MERLOT Journal of Online Teaching and Learning* 6, no. 4 (2010): 839–51; Leora S. Waldner, Sue Y. McGorry, and Murray C. Widener, "E-Service-Learning: The Evolution of Service-Learning to Engage a Growing Online Student Population," *Journal of Higher Education Outreach and Engagement* 16, no. 2 (2012): 123–50.

20. Waldner, McGorry, and Widener, "Extreme E-Service Learning," 844.

21. Kathy L. Guthrie and Holly McCracken, "Teaching and Learning Social Justice Through Online Service-Learning Courses," *International Review of Research in Open and Distance Learning* 11, no. 3 (2010): 79.

22. Waldner, McGorry, and Widener, "Extreme E-Service Learning," 846–47.

23. Waldner, McGorry, and Widener, "E-Service Learning," 139.

24. Jean Strait and Tim Sauer, "Constructural Experiential Learning for Online Courses: The Birth of E-Service," *Educause Quarterly* 27, no. 1 (2004): 62–65.

25. Simone C. O. Conceição and Chip Donahue, "Intentional Design Based on Understanding the Learners, Teachers, and Content," Paper presented at the 28th Annual Conference on Distance Teaching and Learning, Madison, Wisconsin, August 8–10, 2012.

26. Moore and Kearsley, *Distance Education*, 20.

27. Ibid.

28. Guthrie and McCracken, "Teaching and Learning Social Justice," 89.

Index

About the Editors and Authors

EDITORS

Robert W. Glover, University of Maine

Robert W. Glover is an assistant professor of honors and political science at the University of Maine. He studies community engagement, democratic participation, and immigration policy and has published in a wide range of disciplinary journals and edited volumes. He is also an active researcher and innovator in the scholarship of teaching and learning, having co-edited with Daniel Tagliarina the volume *Teaching Politics Beyond the Book: Films, Texts, and New Media in the Classroom* (Bloomsbury Academic, 2012). He is a 2014 recipient of the Douglas Harward Faculty Award for Service Learning Excellence given by the Maine Campus Compact and was recognized by the Maine State Senate for his innovative work fostering undergraduate community-based policy research.

Katherine M. O'Flaherty, Arizona State University

Katherine M. O'Flaherty is an Honors Faculty Fellow at Barrett, the Honors College at Arizona State University. She holds a PhD in history and CAS in higher education leadership from the University of Maine. O'Flaherty primarily researches immigration and refugee history from World War II to the present and has designed several upper-level honors courses that provide students the opportunity to undertake research on immigration-related issues. She also researches and teaches about issues in higher education and the ways technology intersects with teaching and learning in the humanities and the liberal arts. She was selected as a Digital Humanities Award Winner for one of her curated projects in 2013.

CHAPTER AUTHORS

Jaclyn M. Chancey, University of Connecticut

Jaclyn M. Chancey is the assistant director for curriculum, assessment, and planning in the honors program at the University of Connecticut. She holds a PhD in educational psychology from the University of Connecticut with concentrations in gifted and talented education and counseling psychology. She has taught in the Honors College at the University of Alabama and also served in a variety of capacities in their Office of Information Technology. She has published on gifted and talented education in *Psychology in the Schools* and regularly presents at national conferences for the American Educational Research Association and the National Association for Gifted Children.

Jennifer Lease Butts, University of Connecticut

Jennifer Lease Butts is the assistant vice provost for enrichment programs and director of the honors program at the University of Connecticut, a post that she has held since 2012. At the University of Connecticut, she has also served as the director of the Office of Undergraduate Research (2005–2010). She holds a PhD in counseling and human development, student affairs administration from the University of Georgia with a specialty area in gifted education. Her work examining honors students and administration in academic and student affairs has been published in *Advancing Undergraduate Research* (an edited volume published by the Council on Undergraduate Research) as well as in *New Directions for Student Services and the Georgia Journal of College Student Development.*

Daniel Mercier, Wesleyan University

Daniel Mercier is the director of instructional design in the Center for Pedagogical Innovation at Wesleyan University. He was previously with the Institute for Teaching and Learning at the University of Connecticut (1996–2015), most recently serving as the institute's director. He holds a MA in education from the University of Connecticut and has published and presented on a variety of topics in contemporary higher education, including faculty development, curriculum design, and distance education, as well as evaluation and assessment.

Brett Nachman, University of Wisconsin–Madison

Brett Nachman is a PhD student at University of Wisconsin–Madison in its educational leadership and policy analysis program. His fellowship includes researching STEM students at two-year colleges. Nachman serves on the Honor Society of Phi Kappa Phi's National Council of Students. He received his BA in journalism and mass communication from Arizona State University's (ASU) Walter Cronkite School of Journalism and Mass Communication. Nachman also graduated from ASU's Barrett, the Honors College. His interest in studying two-year colleges emerged at Scottsdale Community College, where he obtained his AA in journalism, was the student commencement speaker, and led multiple organizations.

Maureen Kelleher, Northeastern University

Maureen Kelleher was the director of the university honors program at Northeastern University from 2004 to 2014, where she developed a number of program innovations with her honors team. She has served on a number of National Collegiate Honors Council committees focusing on topics including large university issues and global education. She is currently on the NCHC national board. She has recently returned to the Department of Sociology and Anthropology at Northeastern, where she is an associate professor. She has published on honors education in the *Journal of the National Collegiate Honors Council* and *Honors in Practice.* She continues to teach in honors and conducts research on the honors experience on topics including advising and program innovation.

Lauren Pouchak, Northeastern University

Lauren Pouchak is the senior associate director of the university honors program at Northeastern University, a position she has held since 2004. She has published in the *Journal of the National Collegiate Honors Council* and *Honors in Practice*, as well as being highly active in the activities of the National Collegiate Honors Council.

Darren J. Reid, University of Maine

Darren J. Reid served as the inaugural Cohen Research Associate at the University of Maine from January 2014 to June 2015. Prior to this, he served as a communications and project support officer for the Scottish Global Forum in Glasgow, Scotland. He holds a Masters of Research (MRes) degree in global security from the University of Glasgow. In addition, he holds a MA (Hons) degree from the University of Dundee, where his primary fields were political science and international relations. He also served as the editor-in-chief for the *Cohen Journal of Leadership and Democracy*. Darren expects to begin his doctoral studies in Central and Eastern European studies at the University of Glasgow in September 2016.

John Zubizarreta, Columbia College

John Zubizarreta is a professor of English and the director of honors and faculty development at Columbia College. The 2010 Carnegie Foundation/CASE U.S. Professor for Baccalaureate Colleges, he is also the winner of several national and international teaching awards. Among his publications, he is the author of *The Learning Portfolio: Reflective Practice for Improving Student Learning* (second edition, Jossey-Bass, 2009; first edition, Anker, 2004), co-author of *Inspiring Exemplary Teaching and Learning: Perspectives on Teaching Academically Talented College Students* (NCHC, 2008), and *The Robert Frost Encyclopedia* (Greenwood, 2001). He is a past president of NCHC and the Southern Regional Honors Council. He is an NCHC program reviewer and has been the college's honors director for over twenty-five years. He has made presentations and led workshops at many regional, national, and international conferences, delivered keynote addresses worldwide, and collaborated with hundreds of students on panels, publications, and undergraduate research. He serves on NCHC's *Honors in Practice* editorial board and has completed three terms on the board of directors.